# Praise for
## *What Happy Teachers Do*

'Teaching can be a tough job at the best of times; this book will help you get through the more challenging ones and remind you of the difference you make.'

<small>DAVE MCPARTLIN, HEADTEACHER, KEYNOTE SPEAKER AND
WINNER OF *BRITAIN'S GOT TALENT* 2019 GOLDEN BUZZER</small>

'In a world where the demands on educators have never been higher, this book emerges as a beacon of hope and transformation. Drawing from deep personal experience and a passionate commitment to wellbeing, it offers not just strategies but a compass for navigating the complexities of teaching with grace, resilience and an open heart. A must-read for educators seeking not only to survive but to thrive in their careers.'

<small>NICK ORTNER, *NEW YORK TIMES* BESTSELLING AUTHOR OF
*THE TAPPING SOLUTION*</small>

'This book is a lifeline for teachers feeling the weight of their role. Open its pages to alleviate stress and rediscover the joy of teaching. It's a must-read for any educator looking to find balance and enthusiasm in their work again.'

<small>JESSICA ORTNER, *NEW YORK TIMES* BESTSELLING AUTHOR</small>

'The most inspiring teachers I know have a twinkle in their eye; they are inspired and they are following their joy. *What Happy Teachers Do* imparts valuable insights on how to nurture this "joy spark" so as to experience greater meaning and purpose in your vocation.'

<small>ROBERT HOLDEN, BESTSELLING AUTHOR OF
*HAPPINESS NOW!* AND *HIGHER PURPOSE*</small>

T0112951

'THE wellbeing manual for teachers. Crammed with great advice, full of practical ideas and written with love, this book will help you wrestle your life back!'
ANDY COPE PHD, BESTSELLING AUTHOR AND WELLBEING EXPERT

MICHELLE AUTON

# What Happy Teachers Do

### The **Three-Step Self-Care System** to Support You Inside and Outside the Classroom

**HAY HOUSE**

Carlsbad, California • New York City
London • Sydney • New Delhi

**Published in the United Kingdom by:**
Hay House UK Ltd, The Sixth Floor, Watson House
54 Baker Street, London W1U 7BU
Tel: +44 (0)20 3927 7290; www.hayhouse.co.uk

**Published in the United States of America by:**
Hay House LLC, PO Box 5100, Carlsbad, CA 92018-5100
Tel: (1) 760 431 7695 or (800) 654 5126; www.hayhouse.com

**Published in Australia by:**
Hay House Australia Publishing Pty Ltd, 18/36 Ralph St, Alexandria NSW 2015
Tel: (61) 2 9669 4299; www.hayhouse.com.au

**Published in India by:**
Hay House Publishers (India) Pvt Ltd, Muskaan Complex,
Plot No.3, B-2, Vasant Kunj, New Delhi 110 070
Tel: (91) 11 4176 1620; www.hayhouse.co.in

Text © Michelle Auton, 2024

The moral rights of the author have been asserted.

All rights reserved. No part of this book may be reproduced by any mechanical, photographic or electronic process, or in the form of a phonographic recording; nor may it be stored in a retrieval system, transmitted or otherwise be copied for public or private use, other than for 'fair use' as brief quotations embodied in articles and reviews, without prior written permission of the publisher.

The information given in this book should not be treated as a substitute for professional medical advice; always consult a medical practitioner. Any use of information in this book is at the reader's discretion and risk. Neither the author nor the publisher can be held responsible for any loss, claim or damage arising out of the use, or misuse, of the suggestions made, the failure to take medical advice or for any material on third-party websites.

A catalogue record for this book is available from the British Library.

Tradepaper ISBN: 978-1-4019-7813-6
E-book ISBN: 978-1-83782-257-7
Audiobook ISBN: 978-1-83782-256-0

Interior images: © 154: Shutterstock; all other images: 123RF

10 9 8 7 6 5 4 3 2 1

Printed in the United States of America

This product uses responsibly sourced papers and/or recycled materials. For more information, see www.hayhouse.com.

*For Simon, Abi and Jacob*
*xxx*

# Contents

# Introduction

*'Taking care of our physical and emotional health
and wellness never ends. We're not here to find
the finish line – we're here to enjoy the journey.'*

JESSICA ORTNER

I got into teaching, like many, because I wanted to make a
difference and help a child to grow not just academically but as
a whole person.

In 1998, I started my career teaching seven-year-olds in a school
with three forms in each year. It was in Hounslow, West London,
and my classroom was next to a train line and under a flight path
to Heathrow airport. I remember that I had to pause during
teaching when the noise of trains and planes was too loud for
the children to hear what I was saying. We were fortunate to be
close to places of worship for several faiths, and visits and visitors
enriched our curriculum. I have fond memories of parties at the
end of term when we shared food from the many cultures that made
up our school, such as freshly cooked samosas. There was a true
sense of community and I was well supported by two experienced
colleagues who embraced my enthusiasm and nurtured me when

I wasn't sure of something. I feel very lucky to have had them as guides at the start of my career.

But despite their support, I spent much of my early teaching career running on nervous energy. I was always in a rush, with my mind working overtime thinking about all the things I needed to do. This rushing around was made worse because I was always worrying about something. I was having so many exaggerated thoughts that I did not recognize or acknowledge that I was making myself ill.

In my third year of teaching, my husband and I moved, and we started new jobs. I worked in a junior school with three forms per year group, teaching Year 6 (11-year-olds). At the time, the school set children in groups by ability for Maths and English. I can still remember, over 20 years later, the worried thoughts that I had at the time. I felt like an imposter; I could not just look at a piece of work and assess the level of it – which seemed possible for my colleagues.

I remember one incident in particular when I needed to find a suitable text for English to teach over six weeks. Although a few texts were suggested to me, I did not know any of them. I remember taking these texts home in the first week of term and crying, not knowing where to start. I could not read three different 200-page books within a week, decide which one to use and then do all my planning. In those days, we still planned work using books, because the internet was not available to search for options, look at reviews and see what others were planning. I felt like a fraud, that I was not fit to teach, that I would be letting down the children in my class. The exaggerated thoughts came thick and fast, and they were on a constant loop in my head. I felt completely lost and out of my depth.

The niggling thoughts kept coming: that I didn't know enough, that I wasn't experienced enough, that I would let the school down, that they would wonder why they had employed me. The thoughts were crippling. I felt like a nuisance when, in the end, I went to the Head of Year for support. She helped me to select one text to teach the class and reeled off some things she had taught related to the text in the past. It then felt more manageable to be able to read and plan from one book. My anxious thoughts had stopped me from being able to logically think through a problem to a decision. I needed support to know the choice I made would be okay.

## The Ripple Effect

Over the years, I learned how important it is to look after yourself properly and seek support when you need it if you want to be a great teacher. Now, as an Assistant Headteacher, it is my job to support my colleagues. I'm a qualified mindfulness teacher and tapping practitioner (I will explain what this means in Part III), and I lead wellbeing sessions for staff in my own school and in other schools locally, including working with trainee teachers as part of their initial training. I have also worked with groups of children across our school to help them develop strategies for self-regulation and to attain a state of relaxed alertness. We know that when staff and pupils have wellbeing support strategies then pupils are more likely to engage in their best learning.

It helps that for the last 10 years, I have worked in a school that is committed to pupil and staff wellbeing. It's a small state school in Essex, England, where I have taught across the primary phase, from four- to 11-year-olds. We have a mixed economic catchment of pupils, but the ethos and sense of community are something that makes the school unique. Positive wellbeing for staff, pupils and their families is a driving factor in our school because we know that this will have the biggest impact on the experience we provide. Our school pioneered an ongoing project called Agents of Change with the aim of helping pupils realize that small acts of kindness, positivity and action can make a difference. These acts may have a ripple effect that helps others to make a difference too. Frequently, this effect shines through and the pupils demonstrate what it means to them to be part of this community. As part of our Agents of Change project, we encourage our pupils to complete tasks that help them recognize they can improve things for others and create what they hope to see in the world. Some of the tasks, titled Be Still and Eat, Sleep, Move, are about looking after their own wellbeing and they help our pupils recognize the importance of self-care.

We have regular assemblies for the whole school, usually led by a senior member of staff. Sometimes, a small group of children will ask to lead an assembly and one of these was particularly heart-warming. Two pupils aged 10, who had both led an assembly before, invited a seven-year-old boy to join them. The three of them had planned an interactive assembly on how to save the planet. They showed posters they had created, shared suggestions and asked the audience to share some of their ideas. What made the assembly stand out in my mind was how they answered our Headteacher, who asked the older two pupils why they had chosen to lead an assembly. One pupil, who needs support with his learning, explained how he finds it hard to say what he wants to because he struggles with his speech. When he was younger, he had helped his sister present assemblies and he found it helped him feel more confident about speaking. Many of the staff became choked up, as they knew how hard learning and speaking could be for that pupil. The other older child shared how she sometimes finds it hard to come to school, but presenting an assembly makes her feel happy and proud of herself. The youngest child was asked how he felt doing his first assembly. He replied that he had felt nervous, but he was glad he had done it. The older children then offered to help anyone else who wanted help to deliver an assembly and encouraged pupils to find them in the playground at lunchtime. Our pupils demonstrated to us how to be the best version of ourselves, how to push past things that may seem daunting and be proud of ourselves for moving out of our comfort zone.

One small ripple that fills my heart with joy began during an assembly when the school learned that I was writing a book to support teachers. I have loved writing this book; I enjoy the creativity of the process. The mother of one of my pupils then told me that since the assembly her child has been inspired to write his own book, so he can be an author too! Hearing that made my day. In teaching, we do not always get to see the small ripples that we help to create, but when we do it reinforces that teaching really is one of the best jobs. What small ripples might you have started? How can actions that support your wellbeing help someone else?

I want to be an Agent of Change for education – to make a positive difference to teacher wellbeing. I want to celebrate and champion self-care strategies, mindfulness and tapping, because when a teacher has established good wellbeing it ripples out to the classes they teach and the colleagues they work alongside.

# Why Now?

A few years ago, I started to read books by The Art of Brilliance (a company led by Andy Cope that supports schools with positive psychology) and watched online sessions that they led on being your best self by considering your 'why' – your purpose in life. I considered my 'why' for some time before settling on feeling safe, calm and energized and helping others to feel the same way. Another task was to think about your Huge Unbelievable Gigantic Goal (HUGG) and the steps to achieve it.[1] My HUGG was to help others with their wellbeing in schools. At the time I had no idea how I could possibly achieve that. I had previously qualified as a tapping practitioner and had seen the benefits. I set some smaller goals to expand my tapping clients and to train to teach mindfulness. Just over 18 months later, I was a qualified mindfulness teacher for adults and children.

Fast forward to summer 2022 and I was on holiday reading Julia Cameron's book *The Artist's Way*, which invites readers to complete certain tasks each week and daily morning pages, similar to a journal. On the last night of our holiday, I could not sleep because I had so many ideas racing through my mind about how I could write a book to help teachers to reduce stress and have strategies to support their wellbeing. My mind was buzzing and I stayed up all night writing down ideas.

When we arrived home, I read the next chapter of *The Artist's Way*, which encouraged readers to take opportunities as they present themselves. Then I opened my emails to find two messages; one was from EFT International (a tapping organization), sharing information about getting tapping into education – something that I am passionate about. The other email was from Hay House advertising their writer's workshop in Edinburgh, Scotland. It felt like a sign of something I should explore. The workshop was in the second week of the school year, which didn't seem ideal timing, but my husband saw how much I was enjoying writing and encouraged me to buy a ticket and book a flight.

I arrived at the Edinburgh venue not knowing anyone. It did not matter as I found I was soon speaking to people with a shared purpose of developing ideas into books. The energy in the hall of 200 participants was electrifying. I found myself sitting with people who had travelled from all over the world to attend the workshop. Many people had already written their books, had previous books published or had self-published, whereas I had only written a few thousand words. I learned so much from the workshop and left feeling invigorated and motivated. At the end of the workshop, we were encouraged to submit our book proposals to Hay House and they would either offer feedback about how to develop our work or they would publish it. I entered the competition and was shocked to find they wanted to publish my book. I feel incredibly lucky and honoured to have won a publishing contract.

Writing this book has brought me much joy and I hope that my love of writing it translates into a book that brings you kind and gentle support to be a happy teacher in your professional and personal life.

This book has never been more needed. The year 2023 saw the greatest number of teacher strikes in the UK in 15 years. Teachers decided to strike not just about falling pay in real terms, but also about the pressures of unmanageable workloads, staff shortages and the sense of social crisis. Teachers support pupils and their families with their social, emotional and wellbeing needs, so they feel the full force of the cost-of-living crisis from many angles. Add to that the pressures of inspections from external bodies, which put great stress on teachers and school leaders to perform and to celebrate the school in a snapshot view. The impact of school inspections can change the fate of a school in days and can unfortunately ruin careers.

With all the unique pressures and accountability faced by the teaching profession, it's really no wonder that so many teachers feel overwhelmed or judged, and question what they are doing. Many are even considering quitting the profession altogether. Research published by the National Education Union (NEU) in March 2022 reported that 44 per cent of teachers plan to leave the profession within the next five years and 20 per cent of teachers will leave in their first two years of teaching, before their careers have really begun.[2]

There has been much research into the reasons why teachers leave the profession, with one of the main factors being stress. Research conducted by the Department for Education (DfE) in England investigated why teachers are leaving. The report found that:

*'Many teachers reported that workload levels negatively impacted on their ability to maintain an appropriate work–life balance, stress levels and general wellbeing, and that this was the main contributing factor in their decision to leave the profession.'*[3]

There is a dire need for wellbeing support in the education system and it is vital that teachers have self-care strategies to protect their own wellbeing, reduce stress and balance their personal lives with work.

In many parts of the world, schools are literally under attack with bomb threats, gun shootings and kidnappings. It is hard to imagine the levels of stress and anxiety that teachers and their classes face in these situations. It is normal for staff and students to practise procedures about how to stay safe in these situations. My friends who taught in the USA described how during one practice their daughter, who was in her early teens, had been in the bathroom when the practice started, meaning she was locked out of her classroom. Their school had an automatic lockdown on doors, and she had to sit curled up on a toilet seat, hugging her legs, so that if someone looked under the toilet door the cubicle appeared empty. What a terrifying experience for the girl and her teacher who must have been worrying where she was.

## Why We Need Self-Care

A certain amount of stress is good for the body as it can help to motivate us and move us out of our comfort zone. A small amount of stress may help us to achieve things that we were unsure that we could achieve. When we are stressed, our bodies produce adrenaline and cortisol. In small doses, both chemicals in our bodies are useful. They help us to be more focused and have more energy for what we are doing.

However, if we continue to be stressed for prolonged periods of time then our bodies keep producing adrenaline and cortisol and they flood our system, putting us on high alert the whole time. They stop our bodies from functioning at their best and can make us ill. This situation can lead to long-term health problems. When our bodies produce too much cortisol and adrenaline, we produce less serotonin and oxytocin, which help us regulate ourselves.

In my early career, I was under a lot of stress and it manifested physically and psychologically. I was having so many exaggerated thoughts that I wasn't recognizing or acknowledging that I was making myself ill. I used to suffer with stomach pains that made me feel constantly nauseated. My doctor referred me to hospital, where I was placed on medication for the pains that were caused by my stomach producing too much acid. I haven't needed to take any medication for these pains for years, as I've come to realize that it was my level of stress and worry that was making me ill. I would overthink work-related issues to such a degree that I made myself sick.

Even now, there are times that I completely overthink a potential situation. I worry about an upcoming trip or having a difficult conversation with a parent. My mind goes into overdrive and I catastrophize. I think about conversations or scenarios that hopefully will never happen. During these times, I know I'm anxious about a potential situation, but I also know that my thoughts are not helping me.

Exaggerated thoughts often become repetitive – it doesn't seem to matter how much we don't want to think about something, the thought becomes persistent and keeps coming back. We can have the same thoughts thousands of times a day – just saying that sounds exhausting. The same negative, draining thought over and over again. Each time you have that same exaggerated thought your body responds by triggering a nervous energy or discomfort in your body warning you of potential danger. This happens repetitively in your body when these thoughts occur.

Over the years, I have learned that the sooner I address the thoughts that are niggling me, the thoughts that keep coming back, the sooner I feel better. I find that speaking to someone else helps to normalize the perceived problem or worry. Also, I have learned to recognize that these are exaggerated thoughts, that I have emphasized and worried about more than necessary. Once you acknowledge that a thought is exaggerated then you have the power to decide what to do about it. By acknowledging your thoughts, it is also easier to acknowledge how they make you feel. I often feel a nervous energy when I have exaggerated thoughts. I feel it as an unease in my stomach, a fluttering, uncomfortable feeling. Other people may feel it in different places in their bodies, maybe in their chest, arms, or as a tightness in the back of their neck or shoulders. All of us hold our stress and worries in different places and it is helpful to identify them. Once I feel stress in my body, I use two strategies to help my wellbeing: mindfulness and tapping.

I believe that it's imperative that teachers practise self-care. It is true that teaching is a job with a never-ending list of things that need to be completed; however, it is never-ending because teachers are passionate, and they want to make a difference to the pupils they teach. To do this, teachers need to look after themselves. This is similar to when you are on an aircraft and instructed always to fix on your own oxygen mask before helping others with their mask. To enjoy teaching, you need to look after your own basic needs first before you look after others. When we are well in ourselves then teaching becomes a bit easier, more creative and more rewarding.

In a typical primary class in the UK, you are responsible for around 30 children, but you are also supporting their parents and classroom teaching assistants, as well as yourself; this means you could be holding and supporting 100 people's needs each day. If you teach secondary pupils and you are teaching different classes each day, you could be seeing and supporting even more people. When it is expressed like this you can see why you need to take care of yourself!

I think the key to good wellbeing in education is not a huge change in routine, but small considered changes that can build to make a big change. Lots of small steps can make a big difference. This book will provide you with the tools to support your own wellbeing so you can create a bespoke self-care package that helps you feel in control, happy and able to enjoy a balanced life – and continue to do your amazing work.

## How to Use This Book

*What Happy Teachers Do* is a practical guide for teachers to reduce stress and prioritize self-care. It will provide you with strategies for robust self-care, so you feel empowered and enabled to do the job you love. It is primarily aimed at teachers in their first five to eight years of teaching, because this is when many teachers consider leaving the profession and need the most support to feel valued and know if they want to persevere with the profession. However, the tools, strategies and ideas will help all teachers, regardless of how long they have been teaching. Sometimes we all need a reminder about looking after our self-care and help in reducing stress. There may be times in your career when you change schools, have a change in leadership or take on a different role that may result in you feeling vulnerable, and then you need to increase your self-care. We can all feel new or vulnerable at any time in our careers, and having robust self-care strategies can help us ride the waves of transition. This book is organized so that you can read it from cover to cover but you can also dip in and out of it as you need.

The book is split into three parts: self-care, mindfulness and tapping. Each explains related research and how different strategies can support self-care in teaching and in other aspects of life. In the self-care part, I examine the importance of self-care, the value of routines and organization, dealing with challenging behaviour and celebrating what is working well. I address the teaching year with its cyclical nature – I identify the pressure points and how to prepare and manage these periods.

The mindfulness part of the book explains the neuroscience and benefits of mindfulness. I model different short mindful practices that you can implement in times of stress, when you feel overwhelmed, exhausted or judged. I share positive psychology strategies and help you identify what sustains and drains you.

In the tapping section of the book, I explain how to tap and how tapping works. There is a chapter on tapping for various aspects of life, such as difficulty with sleeping and feeling vulnerable, as well as a chapter on tapping for teaching that provides tapping scripts for specific stressors, such as lesson observations and end-of-term tiredness.

Throughout the book, I will share my experiences, and those of my husband (who works in secondary education) and friends who are teachers. I am well aware that every school (possibly every class) is different and that there are many types of school around the world that have different approaches, different curriculums, different challenges and different languages for discussing education. I hope that you are able to relate to our experiences in the UK and use them to create a bespoke wellbeing plan that works for you. All of the strategies I share with you are generic. Please take them as a stimulus and adjust them to benefit you. I invite you to choose the suggestions that appeal to you.

Many chapters include Things to Ponder lists, with questions to reflect on. I invite you to have your own ideas about the content and ideas raised in the book. Many of the areas covered in this book are written in a teaching context; however, I have also included examples of everyday stressors and coping strategies, because I want you to be a happy person, not just a happy teacher. So, this is what happy teachers do.

# PART I

# Self-Care

CHAPTER 1

# The Teaching Year

*'Never underestimate the valuable and
important difference you make in every life
you touch for the impact you make today has
a powerful rippling effect on every tomorrow.'*

LEON BROWN

The teaching year has its own unique rhythm, with mandatory weeks of intense teaching interspersed with school holidays. Recognizing the cyclical nature of the year, with its ebbs and flows, will help us to understand pressure points and consider how to get the best out of ourselves and the students we teach.

In this chapter, we will consider some key milestones in the teaching year, starting with the end of summer holidays and anticipation about the year ahead. We will explore how you can use this time to prepare and plan ways to look after yourself. Next, we will move on to the start of the year, when teachers can quickly go from refreshed to bombarded. We'll talk about how terms often start with a fear of having forgotten how to teach and an ever-lengthening to-do list that has the potential to feel unachievable and overwhelming very quickly. That's where this book comes in – throughout the chapter you'll find tips and ideas to support you, while we celebrate the uniqueness of the teaching year, exploring themes from report writing to whole-school events, up to the end of the academic year.

# The Start of the Academic Year

The final week of the summer holidays is always a strange time for me. At any other point a week of holiday is something to be cherished, something to look forward to and make plans for, but I always find the last week of the summer holidays different. There is a nervous, unsettled energy – I feel a restlessness. The ability to sleep later in the morning disappears as my body prepares itself for the abrupt change that is about to occur. By the end of summer, I have usually lost track of days and the household routines of term time seem long gone. But like an animal coming out of hibernation, I feel the need to return to order. I know that the more prepared our household is in the last week of the holidays, the easier the start of the new school year will be.

As my husband and I are both teachers we have certain things that we do at this time of year, which I'm not sure if we even do consciously. The whole house usually has a deep clean, if it hasn't been done already over the summer. Then the future-proofing begins, starting with batch cooking. Every good term starts with the freezer stocked up with delicious and easy meals for workdays – spaghetti bolognese, chilli, curry and homemade pasta sauce. There is a certain comfort in knowing that even during the busiest of weeks, when we both have crammed schedules or our children have lots going on outside of school, there are easy home-cooked meals that the whole family likes in the freezer. We also have meal planners on a four-week cycle. While this may seem overly organized, it makes our term-time lives much easier and minimizes our food waste. We know what to buy in the weekly shop and there is still variety in our meals. Each morning before work, we take food out of the freezer to defrost so whoever is home first can get dinner ready easily and quickly.

Also, at this time of year, I often start to overthink and my self-doubt rears up. There is a certain amount of imposter syndrome that creeps in before the start of the school year for many teachers. In the last few years, I have tried doing things differently. I've spoken openly to other staff about self-doubt and found that they feel the same way. Many of them were surprised when we had an open conversation about the issue, and it became something we could laugh about together. We all knew that by lunchtime of the first day of term we would remember that of course we can still teach, and we do know what to do. Some anxiety probably comes from the need to completely turn off during the summer so that you are relaxed and ready for the new academic year. Another factor is the deep desire to do the absolute best for the children you teach.

Recently, I rewrote most of my schemes of work for a year group I had taught for the previous five years. I did this partly because we had remodelled the curriculum, but also because I wanted to keep improving and building on what I've taught before. It is important to feel excited about what you are teaching so your enthusiasm is passed on to the children you teach. I spent extra time planning for the first few weeks of term because I wanted to try a slightly different approach. I knew I had spent longer than necessary because I was aiming for something better – this is not a sustainable way of working but it helped me to feel calmer about trying something different.

There is a certain amount of self-reflection that happens in this transition time between the holidays and the new school year. I feel rested, my mind is not overstimulated and I find myself thinking about how this year could be different. I consider changes I could make to ensure that I feel balanced between work and home life, to feel that I have energy left at the end of the day to exercise and nurture myself and my family. This is when I find myself setting optimistic goals – in the hope that if I keep doing the things that make me feel good then I will not get ill, stressed or overwhelmed. My plan usually goes something like… this year I will leave work by a reasonable time two nights a week to ensure I spend quality time with my family, or I will not overstretch myself in what I can do in a day, or I will start each day with a yoga session and meditation.

These targets are completely achievable, but I find that however much I want to prioritize them at the start of term, they can drop off when everything else kicks in. I know that I am setting myself these targets because they do make a massive difference to my mental health and wellbeing. I know that when I have practised yoga, tapped or meditated before school starts, my day proceeds in a much nicer and calmer way. Everything is less overwhelming and there is a sense of achievement, of doing something for myself before the rest of my house is even stirring. The drive to work on those days is less pressured, I am less bothered by traffic conditions or journey times. If bringing these small practices into my day affects how I feel about my journey then I predict it will have a positive impact later, on my interactions with my class, parents and other staff.

The key is not to feel that any practice is something you must do every day. Celebrate the days when you have managed to achieve your wellbeing goals and be kind to yourself when you did not do what you hoped. There is often a reason why you could not practise your wellbeing aim: Maybe your child needed more help than usual in the morning, or you didn't get up as soon as the alarm went off. The key is finding a balance – see it as a win when you manage to practise and something to aim for when you don't. I chose to continue with my optimistic goal-setting this year.

It is okay to have times of heightened stress, as stress can be a useful motivator and can help to push us out of our comfort zone. I think it is important to recognize when we are stressed and notice the reasons for it. There will also be times when we get sick. Working in a school environment, where teachers have close contact with many children, there is a greater chance of picking up an illness. We are more likely to become ill if we are run down or feeling low, so having our optimistic goals in mind and being aware of our own feelings and stressors is important.

Some teachers need to work a second job over the summer and do not have the opportunity to rest and recharge before going back to school. The length of summer breaks and how teachers are paid varies in different countries around the world. Having systems in place to nurture yourself and look after your wellbeing is important, whatever situation you are in.

## THINGS TO PONDER

- How do you feel at the end of the holidays?
- What can you do to help protect yourself at the start of term?
- Who can you talk to about how you are feeling?
- What optimistic goals are you going to set for yourself?

# Mapping Your Term

The school term can be viewed like a marathon: It needs planning and thinking about the best strategy to cross the finishing line without collapsing. We may have different strategies because we all approach things in different ways. However, with some thought, we can pace ourselves and enjoy the journey.

Having an overview of the term or half term and what is coming up can help you plan some highly motivating activities each week without them being too overwhelming for you or your class. If every lesson were a WOW, multisensory, high-energy lesson then both you and your class would be exhausted. This is where your strategy starts to unfold – map in the things that have already been decided for you, such as whole-school projects or visitors. Next, consider if these events need preparation with your class; for example, if you have a visitor coming in to deliver a talk, do you need to factor in time to consider questions that your class might ask? Do the children need some background about what is being discussed so they can get more out of the event? Do the children need time to talk about what is going to happen? They may need some reassurance before the event if it is a new experience for them.

Thinking through all aspects and planning in time to do any preparation with your class will enable the children to get the most out of the experience or event, as well as help them feel secure and safe when embracing new challenges. In turn, this preparation helps your self-care because a secure, safe class environment feels safer and securer for you too. All teachers have the primary aim of wanting the best for the children they teach, so when you know that you have considered what is best for your class you will feel better in yourself, too.

Once any predetermined events or activities have been mapped in, you can look at your curriculum and timetable to see how best to plan the term. If you're a primary school teacher and you have a fully practical Science lesson and a messy, fun Art lesson, then you may want to balance them with a calmer Geography lesson. If all lessons are all singing and dancing, then you will become exhausted, and it will be too overwhelming for your class. Too much stimulation can be triggering for some children. If you can work flexibly with your class timetabling, I find it helps to block a subject or unit for a week of work, so the children become fully immersed in the learning without having to wait until the following week for the next part of the unit. It can also save you time, as you can plan and get resources ready for the unit rather than getting them out and putting them away after each lesson. If you teach secondary school pupils, you may find it easier to plan one complete week at a time so you know you have all lessons ready before the week starts – this can ensure you have balance in what you want to teach.

It can be helpful to think about your self-care in a comparable way to how you plan for the term or half term. Think about your week ahead and consider what self-care you are going to make sure that you include for yourself. Think about which times of day are best for you to have some time for yourself or when you will do things that make you feel good about yourself. Now that my children are teenagers, I find that first thing in the morning is a good time to be undisturbed and do what I would like to do. I usually start my morning with some tapping and will then do either some yoga, some writing, a workout, some karate practice or a meditation. I know that if I find the time to do any of these activities then I will feel better in myself, and my wellbeing bucket will have been topped up.

You may find a different time of day is better for you – it might be that straight after work is a time when you can build in self-care. This time might work well as a transition period between school and home. Or it may be that later in the evening works as a time for you to do things that you know make you feel good.

It is worth having a plan about what you would like to do to look after yourself, because this will mean you are more likely to remember to do it and continue to do it. Regular short bursts of activities that nurture you can make an enormous difference to your whole day.

## THINGS TO PONDER

- What time of day is it easiest to practise self-care?
- Write down five self-care activities that you enjoy and would like to either continue doing or add to your day.

# From Refreshed to Bombarded!

Within two weeks of the start of term, I find that my initial energy and zest have started to fade as my list of jobs grows ever longer. The start of the school year is always full of energy, both nervous and excited energy. Teachers and children alike want to forge new relationships. As teachers, we are keen to establish routines and instil expectations of student behaviour because we know this will help to create the calmest and most-productive learning environment, where children feel nurtured, safe and excited to learn. Laying these foundations always pays dividends, as children settle in quickly.

Our intention is to do the best for the children we teach but it can be tiring. I find myself using vast amounts of energy while I try to get everything right for a new class of children. I want them to know that I really care about them. At the same time, it is important to think about how you may care for yourself. I have heard from colleagues, and experienced myself, that sleep patterns often change during the first few weeks of term. Our minds may be on high alert during this stage of setting expectations with a class and it can then affect our sleep. I have found that I can get to sleep but often wake up in the night with ideas running through my mind. Over the years I have tried various techniques to help me go back to sleep and one that I come back to repeatedly is gratitude. Thinking about things that I am grateful for, and listing them in my head, quietens the thinking mind and allows calmer thoughts to settle me.

No matter how organized you are at the start of term there will be a list of jobs that seems to pile up within the first half term, such as completing initial assessments, reviewing special-needs plans, displaying children's work so they feel valued, whole-school projects and many communications with parents.

## THINGS TO PONDER

-   What items on your list of jobs will have the most impact?

-   What things that you need to do can wait until later in the term?

# Communicating with Parents

Understandably, at the start of the new school year parents have a certain amount of anxiety about their child going into the next stage of their school life. You will have questions from parents; they want to know that you will care for their child and that if they have a concern they will be heard. There are some easy things that we can do to reassure parents that we want the best for their children and that we wish to work in partnership with them. One of the ways you may reassure parents is by writing to them in the first couple of days of term. Let them know how well the class has settled and include a small amount of information about what their child has been learning. Share some key information such as the Physical Exercise (PE) days, when reading books will be changed and arrangements for collecting and dropping off children at school. Let parents know that you have an open-door policy; if they have a concern then they should communicate it to you so it can be addressed quickly. This communication could be through a short letter, email or a school communication app.

You may consider inviting parents into class at collection time one day straight after school so their child can give them a tour of the classroom. Their child may show them what is important to them about the classroom, such as where they sit, where they keep their things and if they have any work on display. Depending on the age group you are teaching, you may need to coach the children about what they could show their parents. You may want to do this a few weeks into the start of the new term, when you have had the opportunity to put children's work on display. Ensuring that every child has something displayed is important, so they all have a piece to be proud of and show their parents.

Another way of reassuring parents is by telling them about the things that their children have done well. When parents pick up their child it is often possible to share something you have observed that day, such as good concentration during a lesson, sharing ideas with the class, expressive reading or being kind when a classmate was upset. These short feedback reports help to reassure parents that you notice their child and care about them. It also helps parents celebrate something positive with their child.

## THINGS TO PONDER

- What can you do to help parents feel reassured that you are looking after their child?

- What is the easiest way for you to communicate with parents?

## Initial Assessments

Pacing initial pupil assessments can help your workload. The pupil's last teacher or education setting, dependent on age, should provide you with assessment data about each child's previous educational attainment levels. When you begin your assessments, try concentrating on one area at a time. Reading is always a good focus for the first week of term, because making time to listen to each child read allows you to quickly see their confidence levels and gives you one-to-one time with them. An unaided piece of writing does not take long to do but can take much longer to assess, so planning when you are going to do this is helpful. Timetabling when you do assessments means that you can feel more organized and less pressured.

Baseline assessments are often used in secondary schools to help with setting and understanding pupil needs. Many secondary schools will have assessment periods scheduled into the school year.

The test-based culture in education varies in different countries around the world. In the UK and USA it can result in a greater need to support pupils' mental health. Being sensitive to this when completing assessments can help pupils develop mental-health strategies from an early age.

# Nearly Holiday Time

By about the fifth week of term, when you are in the full swing of teaching and your topics for the term are established, you may find that you hit an invisible wall. Teachers know that they are not quite at the end of term, but already they feel tired. I have heard staff say how tired they feel so many times while in the staffroom or waiting by the photocopier. They say how much harder it is to get out of bed in the morning, knowing that there are still a few weeks until the holiday. There tends to be more illness at this time and morale can start to dip. This is a good time to reflect on how much you have achieved that term already. Think about how much progress the children have made, be it progress with routines, social interactions, listening skills or anything else.

It is easy for us to get sucked into conversations about feeling tired. Although it is important to recognize and acknowledge how we feel, try not to become consumed by these thoughts. Focusing on how far we or our pupils have reached at this point can be powerful. Knowing that what we do makes a difference can change our mindset from feeling tired to feeling proud. Our energy has been well spent because we have had an influence on others. Next time you feel yourself thinking, *I'm so tired*, why not try adding, *because I have used my energy to make a difference.*

## Listening to Your Body

It is important to listen to your body and what it needs; it will send you signals when you need to rest or take a break. I find it harder to listen to these signals at the end of term when I am shattered, so it is important for me to completely stop during the holidays and make time to recharge my body. I really enjoy the slower start to the days and the opportunity to do things at a steady pace.

During the holidays it is important to do things that fill your cup of wellbeing and make you happy, things you really enjoy doing. For me, that means spending quality time with my family, having a day out or time dedicated to being together. Also, it is great to make time to be with friends and have a change to term-time life. You may just enjoy having time to read a book you've been wanting to read or to do a project that makes you happy. Make time to do the things that make you feel good and help you to relax.

We can become ill when we have been working hard, pushing ourselves to get to the end of term and ignoring warning signs that our body is tired. Quite often teachers and teaching assistants find that they are ill during the holidays, stopping them from doing things they were looking forward to and had planned. It is important to listen to your body rather than push through. Often, we get ill because our body is telling us to stop and we do not listen.

We all become tired at the end of term; it is part of the reason we need longer holidays in education. During term time we work hard, giving it our all and we need time to recharge to do it all again the following term. It helps if we can nurture ourselves nearer the end of term by having earlier nights to get more sleep, by having some quieter weekends when we can refresh and by eating foods that support our wellbeing.

During the holidays I find it is helpful to have days when I have nothing planned or something small, like a coffee with a friend. I know that I need time to slow down completely and function at a different pace to term time. I used to do a lot in the holidays, trying to make the most of every day, especially when my children were younger, but I found it was too much for me and for my children. We all benefitted from having some lazy, chilled days when we did not need to be anywhere and we could all choose how we spent our time at home.

## Parent Consultations

The weeks when we have parent consultations can feel more overwhelming than other weeks. We know that we will be working extended days, when we may have taught all day, had a short break, and then have back-to-back appointments. With each new set of parents there is a need to be welcoming, calm, professional and alert. In reality, by the time you are meeting the 12th set of parents, your mind is not going to be as refreshed.

You cannot be sure of what parents are going to bring to the meeting, but you have a set amount of time to address any queries or concerns as well as share the child's progress. Often parents store up concerns for these consultations, even if the school has an open-door policy actively encouraging parents to talk whenever they have anything on their mind about their child.

At the start of each appointment, I always ask parents if there is anything they would like to share or discuss. If they have concerns that will take longer than the allocated time, I will offer them another meeting at a separate time. It is easier to do this than to delay all the other appointments. Understandably, parents will become frustrated if they have to wait for a long time past their allocated slot, which can easily happen if each appointment overruns. Parents may need to meet with other teachers if they have more than one child in the school. It can also throw another teacher's schedule off if you run late for your appointments. The time pressure is another reason that consultations can feel tiring, as you constantly need to keep an eye on the time and pace of each meeting.

Looking after yourself during the period of parent consultations can make a significant difference. Make sure you have a hearty lunch and that you stay well hydrated each day. Think about your teaching and unless you have time to mark all the children's work before the meeting, I suggest either doing work that can be self-marked or peer-marked, or work that can be done on paper and stuck into the pupil's books the following day. Alternatively, plan lessons that are more active and without any marking, such as some outdoor learning, role play or creative work.

Remember that parents are often nervous about attending consultations. They do not know what you are going to say to them; they only know what their child has told them. Sometimes when a person is nervous, they may come across as defensive.

Starting each consultation with a smile and a friendly welcome can help parents relax and make appointments flow easily. I always end each appointment by reassuring parents that if they have any concerns at any time then they should speak to us or email, so we can help them as soon as possible.

## Seasonal Events

Schools timetable events that vary in size and theme for the entire school. My school often timetables a whole-school event each term. For one event, every child in the school painted a stone that was then placed around a tree in the village to create an art installation. The stones were decorated with positive images and messages. Over the week that followed, the stones were collected and distributed around the village by people in the community choosing a stone they were drawn to and then placing it elsewhere for someone else to find. Whole-school projects can be a great way to unite the school community. A few of our projects have been art based, with the individual efforts of each pupil forming part of a larger piece.

Your school may recognize the Chinese New Year with large assemblies and dragon dances. The event may provide an opportunity for pupils to try cultural activities linked to the Chinese New Year such as learning about tea ceremonies, hearing traditional Chinese stories or trying to write Chinese characters. As a school you may celebrate Diwali, the festival of light, by trying mehndi hand decoration or creating mandalas using chalk and stones, or watching and trying Indian dancing.

For anyone who works in a primary school that celebrates Christmas, the school performance is a special occasion, when even the Grinch would find Christmas cheer. It is a time when everyone across the school comes together to celebrate the performance of the Christmas story. In my school, the six- and seven-year-olds act in the nativity play, with younger children performing a dance and singing a song.

As the teacher of these year groups, Christmas is a magical but often pressurized time. My aim is for all the children in my class to enjoy being on stage and performing. There are always funny situations during the nativity – from Joseph needing the bathroom in the middle of a performance to someone enthusiastically singing louder than everyone else. The tea-towel headdresses invariably fall to one side and the sleepy sheep snore loudly at the wrong time. Someone adds in their own dance moves to the choreographed routine, or the sound system doesn't work. It is all part of the fun.

One year we did a dress rehearsal to the school, where many things seemed to go wrong. It started with the child who was playing Mary taking baby Jesus on stage for the opening song before the story had been told. I crept onto the stage, in front of the whole school, to take the doll from her while all the staff stifled giggles as they realized what had happened. When it was time in the play for Jesus to be born, the doll was dropped on its head before going on stage. Children forgot when it was their time to go on stage, with one child hiding behind another to say his line. Someone sat down in the middle of the stage just before a whole-class dance and needed coaxing to stand up. The children were so enthusiastic to sing that they sang faster than the music. One child's headdress came off and he swung it round like a lasso while doing Makaton signs to one of the songs.

When it finished, I initially felt a bit disappointed as I knew they had performed better in rehearsals. It is easy for us to feel judged if our class does not do something as we had hoped. However, the children had tried their best and had a positive first experience on stage, with much clapping and support from the school. I praised them highly for their hard work, their clear voices and their great singing and dancing. Several members of staff commented that it was just how a nativity was supposed to be! It will certainly be a performance to remember, so they are right: It is how a nativity should be – one full of the children having a memorable experience where they feel good about themselves. It is important to remember the key reason for doing the performance and that the staff at your school are there to support you. It makes me feel incredibly lucky to have that support and people to remind me what really is important.

There can be high-pressured moments, too – when parents decide their child does not have enough lines or when, during rehearsals, you question if it will work on the day. It takes a team to perform a play, but it creates a magical feeling around the entire school. It is important to look after yourself and try and keep things in perspective when it comes to any school performance. Remember the main motivating factor for putting on a performance – for the children to have a fun and engaging experience acting, singing and dancing on stage. Performances help to build children's confidence and try something that they may not have experienced before. The children will notice if teachers are stressed and try to make the play perfect. It does not need to be perfect, but the children do need to enjoy the experience.

Any teacher who has been involved in a school performance will understand how much work and effort it takes, so you can help yourself by asking colleagues for support. As I said earlier, it takes a team to create a performance so ask others to help. It is not a sign of weakness but a way to make everyone feel involved.

Any time you are doing something in school where parents are invited can feel pressurized, but it helps to remember that the parents just want to see their child have their time to shine. Parents want their children to be happy and they would like the opportunity to see them perform. When you keep this in mind it can be easier to deal with parental responses.

The final form in our primary school has an end-of-year performance that is part of their transition before leaving the school. It is a time for the children to excel and work on something different; sometimes they help to write part of the script, as well as helping to design and make props, backdrops and costumes. They have a wider role than the younger children, helping them to understand more about all the elements that go into producing a play.

Colleagues told me about a production of the musical Footloose by secondary pupils where much time and effort had gone into rehearsals and creating a professional-looking performance. It came to the last night of the performance and the tickets were sold out, but the school lost all power! Decisions had to be made – whether to try and carry on without music and lighting, which did not seem fair on anyone, or to reschedule it for a later date, as they decided to do. Sometimes things happen that are out of our control and it is important to talk through options with a senior member of staff and agree on a plan. It is important to recognize that not everyone may be happy with the chosen outcome. In this example, parents would have taken time off work to watch the play that then needed to be rescheduled. Recognizing the feelings of others and acknowledging them is important, but if you have a strong plan, you know that you are doing the best for the pupils.

Do not underestimate the time, effort and enthusiasm it takes to get a group of pupils to perform a play. If you find yourself feeling tired, it is not surprising. It is also one of the most rewarding times in school, when the pupils are beaming with pride after a performance. You are helping to teach the skills of perseverance, teamwork and appreciation of the arts.

## THINGS TO PONDER

- Who in your school team will support you?

- What can you do to make this experience enjoyable and manageable for all, including yourself?

# Sports Day

Sports days are often whole-school events and come with a mix of high excitement and organization. Some schools will run an extremely competitive sports day, some will have a sports day where participation is celebrated and some schools will be somewhere between these models. As parents are often invited, it tends to be a higher-profile event. As a class teacher, you can feel pressure as you try to organize your pupils while their parents are watching. Some children find sports day overwhelming because they know their parents are there and it feels different to a normal day in school. Sport may not be something they excel at, or it may be that they are good at sports but put pressure on themselves to do well. Class teachers hold all the children's emotions while looking professional and keeping everything running smoothly.

Sports days are often organized in the summer term and can be weather dependent. We have had sports days where everyone needed to huddle under trees as it poured down with rain and other sports days where it was so hot that we needed to ensure everyone kept a hat on, drank lots of water and had time in the shade. The mix of unknown variables, whilst feeling watched by parents, can make sports day a time that some teachers do not look forward to.

To help yourself and your class enjoy sports day, think about ways you can make it as stress-free as possible. Find out how the day will be organized. Know the events that the children will be doing and give them an opportunity to practise them in PE lessons. Remind the children how the day will run and let them know if they need to bring anything to school. It is also useful to communicate this information to parents, who can talk about the event with their children at home. Some parents may come in before sports day to share that their child is worried, so it helps parents reassure their child if they know what is going to happen. If there will be team games, let the children know which teams they will be in before the day.

In American schools and colleges there is often an emphasis on sports, and sporting events sometimes draw crowds of thousands to watch them. Students can get scholarships based on sporting ability and ranking. There may be huge pressure on students to maintain or improve their ranking in sport but also to achieve good grade point averages for their academic work. If these scores fall then students may be dropped from sports teams or they may lose scholarships. The pressure students face means they need emotional and mental support from schools. This puts pressure on American teachers to ensure their pupils can secure their grade point average and progress in their education.

## THINGS TO PONDER

- Do you know the format of your sports day?

- What can you do to support yourself and your class to enjoy sports day?

# Residential Trips

Overnight trips can be a source of anxiety both for teachers and students. My husband has run his school's residential trip for 11- and 12-year-old students for the past 15 years. It is a week of the year that he loves, because he likes to see children enjoying themselves, pushing their limits and having fun at the end of their first year of secondary school. He knows they will try things they haven't done before and they will feel a sense of achievement, whether that is climbing on high ropes, capsizing a kayak or staying away from home for the first time. He has many tales of amazing pupil achievements from these residential weeks.

The week away, living in tents, takes many months of planning and organizing, often with a frantic push near the end to make sure everything is ready. He leads meetings with pupils, parents, staff accompanying the trip and student ambassadors from older years. He puts in many hours because he thrives from doing it and he knows it makes a difference to the pupils in his school.

One girl was extremely nervous about attending a school residential, and my husband had spoken to her parents, who also had concerns. It was agreed that for the first day, she would attend during the day but then go home at night. She had such a positive first day that she chose to stay for the rest of the week. It was her birthday during the week, and this had been the source of some of her anxiety about being away from home. Her dad's work involved flying helicopters and as a surprise to wish her happy birthday he flew a helicopter over the main camp – dipping and turning. The girl was overjoyed with this act of love.

One year, while living in tents for the week, there was a huge storm. The rain lashed down and the wind speeds became dangerous. The staff collaboratively worked together to get the children to safety in static buildings, while rivers of water flowed through the tents. All activities had to be cancelled and staff rallied to keep students calm and entertained. These kinds of events are extremely rare and cannot be planned for; however, having a team of staff that you trust and can rely on means that you can deal with situations as they arise.

In another instance, a pupil slipped and hurt their ankle. They had been looking forward to completing a bush-tucker trial, where there are different levels of eating challenges that pupils work together in teams to try to complete. The hardest of the challenges was eating a tarantula leg! The pupil was due to have the bush-tucker activity later in the day, but their ankle injury meant their parents needed to collect them to be checked out at the hospital. While they waited for the parents to arrive, the activity leader and the rest of their team gathered outside the medical tent and completed the trial with the injured pupil. They were delighted when their parents arrived and they told them they had been chosen to eat a tarantula leg! Many of the examples my husband recalls show teams pulling together and supporting each other to help groups or individuals in times of distress or achievement.

## The End of the School Year

The end of the school year is always extremely busy. You are thinking about two classes – your current class and the one you are about to inherit. This means there is much to consider and plan for when you are probably at your most tired. You may need to change classrooms over the summer and that means you must completely strip and pack up the room you are in and prepare your new room. There is always a fine balance when trying to get everything moved at the same time. You may be very organized and use a classroom move as an ideal opportunity to clear through your resources and have a fresh start, or you may be someone who likes to collect their resources in case you need them later, therefore having lots to move.

As the end of term approaches ensure all assessments are up to date, ready to pass on to the next teacher. It is worth spending time considering what would be useful for the next teacher to know about your class. Of course, they need to know the ability of the children, but it is also important to pass on information about medical conditions, or a child's home life, especially if there is anything concerning. It is good to share what the children enjoy, their friends and anything that concerns them. You know your class so well by the end of the year, often knowing their pets' names, their likely choice of sandwich filling, what sports clubs they enjoy and who picks them up from school each day of the week.

The new teacher for your class is unlikely to want old test papers or finished workbooks, but they will want to know the current academic level of each pupil and if they struggle with or excel at anything specific. This information will help the next teacher with their planning for the start of term.

It is important to look after yourself as the end of the school year approaches. The lists of jobs you need to do will be long and can seem overwhelming. It is worth prioritizing what you really need to do. Sorting through your resources earlier in the term will help, or try to develop the habit of filing or binning resources as you go. If you are going to use a resource again then it is worth keeping. If you are not sure, then consider just keeping an electronic version of the resource.

When you take down displays, think about whether the lettering or labels can be used again, as this will save you time next year. Some resources take quite a bit of time to prepare but can be used year after year. You can be prepared and stagger these jobs over the summer term so that you feel more organized.

Make sure you care for yourself during this busy period by taking time to go outside; maybe after leaving work you could go for a walk in nature so you have time to switch off before returning home. You might enjoy having drinks with friends or reading a book in the garden. Make time to do things that you enjoy and find relaxing. Try to be kind to yourself; you will be tired, and the summer term is often long.

The end of the school year also brings celebrations for pupils leaving the school or graduating. It is a time to celebrate and recognize the achievements of pupils – it is a symbolic time. In the USA, schools may hire local sports stadiums for big public celebrations for the students. Parents often have signs in their gardens or yards to celebrate their child's graduation. It is a time when the school is on show and celebrates what is great about it. It is also when staff need to pull together to help create a successful event.

## THINGS TO PONDER

-   What would you like the next teacher of your pupils to know about them as individuals?

-   How are you going to take care of yourself at the end of the school year?

# CHAPTER 2

# Everyday Teaching

*'Success doesn't come from what
you do occasionally, it comes from
what you do consistently.'*

MARIE FORLEO

How organized and planned you are will have an impact on your teaching and how you feel about your work. In this chapter, we think about the importance of routines for the children to feel secure and for you to know what is coming next.

I will encourage you to be positive about your teaching experiences by celebrating small wins both in the classroom and outside. Many circumstances that occur in a classroom may cause frustration; however, if we can find humour in the situation, the frustration dissipates.

We will discuss dealing with challenging behaviour and the impact it can have on teacher wellbeing, the ethos of the school and learning environment for other pupils over time.

# Organization

Being organized as a teacher makes your life so much easier. When my children were young, I remember having this desire and need to work as efficiently as possible so that I felt like I was doing a good job in school and being present at home. I did not like feeling I was trying hard in all aspects of my life, but that I was doing a sub-standard job everywhere. I knew that I did not want to spend a long time doing schoolwork after work at home, as that time was for my children. I had to find a smarter, more-efficient way of working. Being organized is the key to working more efficiently. I also needed to know that if something unexpected happened – if one of my children was poorly, the childminder was ill, we were running late, I had car trouble or any other delay – I had everything ready to teach for the day.

To organize my primary classroom, I:

- have all the resources for Maths, English and phonics prepared before I leave school the previous week

- have one classroom drawer for Maths and one for English. In each drawer, I have five plastic pockets labelled Monday to Friday that I use for the week's resources.

- print learning objectives onto stickers to go into the children's books. I do not date the objectives because if as a class we need to spend longer on a topic than initially planned, the stickers are not wasted.

- train the children to stick in their own objectives

- organize children's workbooks into table groups so the books can be handed out and collected in as quickly and efficiently as possible. The children enjoy having the responsibility of doing this for their small group.

- ask the children to leave their books either open to the page they have been working on if their work has not been marked, or closed in a pile if it has been marked

- use immediate marking whenever possible

- alphabetically label all coat pegs and children's trays so when I or anyone else wants to return something to a child or find a lost item, then it is easy to do quickly

- have class lists for tracking things like awards and the letters sent home

My husband has been teaching secondary pupils for over 20 years; to be efficient, he:

- has lessons planned for the week

- has paper resources printed and organized into lesson files

- has all his slides for the day open on the computer or laptop

- has a bank of lesson opening and ending activities that he can rotate, to recap and reinforce learning

- keeps a zipped wallet of spare stationery resources for pupils to borrow if they need to, such as pens, pencils, glue and rulers

- has book monitors to hand out books while he takes the register to save time

- displays objectives on the first slide of the lesson for pupils to record in their books

- has a rota in his diary for collecting and marking work

- links marking to the school assessment calendar and upcoming parent consultations

- uses peer marking when appropriate

- uses immediate marking during lessons

- sticks resources into workbooks for lower-ability sets before the lesson

- uses technology to set automatically marked homework; for example, quizzes that give instant feedback

## THINGS TO PONDER

– What small steps can you take to be more organized?

# Establishing a Routine

A routine helps children feel more secure and safe in school. It also helps with organization and supports any adults working in the classroom to anticipate what is happening next. Display a visual timetable so the children know what they are going to be doing that day and they will gradually develop a sense of time. Routines also help teachers to work more efficiently, because it is easier to be prepared and organized for the day with a schedule in place.

To establish a routine, you need to know what you need to teach each week, taking into consideration schedules across the whole school such as assemblies, breaks and lunchtimes. You also need to consider subjects that may need different teachers or environments, such as PE and Computing, or if you have a specialist teacher working with your class at a particular time. It is not possible to teach every subject in depth every week, so I find teaching subjects such as Geography, History and Design Technology in a block on rotation works well. If you have time to continue teaching a subject the next day, you can go deeper than if you have to wait until the following week.

In recent years I have mapped out lessons for half a term in subjects other than English and Maths to ensure that I have a good coverage overall. This map only ever acts as a guide, because different things will crop up and I need to be flexible and adapt it when necessary.

My routine usually starts with setting early morning work – an activity to help the children transition into the school day that gives me time to take the register. I often use a Maths activity for early morning work, maybe five questions to reinforce different maths concepts. These are usually questions that the children can work on independently, allowing me time to help any children or parents who have had a tricky start to the day.

Personally, I think it is important for children to have some kind of physical activity built into each school day, so on days when PE is not scheduled I will implement the daily mile as part of our routine. The daily mile is an initiative to ensure that children move a mile each day by either walking, jogging, running or skipping around the playground. This exercise provides an opportunity for children to let off steam in a controlled way. I let the children choose how they wish to travel, as long as they keep moving for 10 to 15 minutes. The daily mile provides time for the children to develop a more relaxed relationship with adults in the class and their peers. They enjoy walking around chatting about what is going on in their lives and what they are looking forward to doing. It is often in these conversations that a teacher may help alleviate any worries and discover what is important to individual children.

## THINGS TO PONDER

- What does your routine look like?

- How do you share class routines with the class?

# Overwhelming Moments

There are times when teaching can feel overwhelming – when you may feel like you are working every hour you are awake, you are putting all your energy into your job and still it seems impossible to get everything done. When teaching feels like this it is exhausting, and you will feel completely drained. It may be that you are in the middle of an assessment cycle, which you know will involve lots of marking, but you also need to plan the next unit of work you are teaching, or you need to do a special-needs review or change classroom displays. You may have a lesson observation, a learning walk to monitor the school learning environment or work scrutiny coming up and it all feels too much. All these things are part of the school year and they come around regularly. You may find sometimes you are fine with whatever is happening and what you need to do, and sometimes it feels too much.

The most important thing to do when you feel overwhelmed is to talk to someone about how you are feeling. If possible, approach someone on the senior leadership team and tell them that you are finding everything too much and that it is hard to cope and get everything done. I know it is difficult to be vulnerable and share how you are feeling, and you may worry that you are going to be judged, but please know that everyone has felt like this at some point in their teaching career, if not multiple times.

Unfortunately, overwhelming times are common in teaching, as the list of jobs is never-ending. When you talk to someone on the senior leadership team, hopefully they will listen carefully to what you say and help you to find ways to make things easier. They may help you prioritize what to do or help you realize something you have seen as a big task can be split into smaller, manageable tasks or left altogether. Having a different perspective on a situation really helps. I find it useful to keep in mind that these feelings of being overwhelmed will pass when you speak to someone.

Sometimes it is hard to know what to let go of, and what jobs you do not need to do. As we mentioned earlier, it is not possible to complete everything on a teaching to-do list as it is never-ending. When we get overloaded or overwhelmed we forget this, and we try to do everything when our energy levels are already depleted. When you are not sure what to prioritize, choose the things that will have the biggest impact on supporting your wellbeing, as when you feel better you will find it easier to focus on what has the most impact on pupil learning. The tasks that have the least impact on your wellbeing and on pupil learning should go to the bottom of the list. These tasks will keep going to the bottom of the list, and that is okay. If the tasks are not supporting you or the children you teach, maybe you need to question whether they are beneficial. It may be they are something for the wider school community or to help with tracking and monitoring in the school. Whatever these other tasks are, they cannot take priority when you are feeling overloaded or overwhelmed.

## THINGS TO PONDER

- Who can you talk to if you feel overwhelmed or overloaded?

- What can you do to support your wellbeing today?

## Come to Me with Solutions!

When I was in my third year of teaching, I moved to a new area and changed the school I worked in. I moved to a three-form entry junior school for seven- to 11-year-olds, and I was made the Head of Year to cover maternity leave. I was responsible for checking data for the year group and feeding it back to the senior leadership team. When problems arose connected to organization or staffing, I reported to the Headteacher, who had been at the school for a long time. He would listen to the problem and then say, 'Don't come to me with problems, come to me with solutions.'

At the time I was flummoxed – I was going to the Headteacher because I was unsure what to do. What he taught me was that I needed to think these problems through myself and consider different options. He did not have a magic wand to change a problem, but he would listen to the different solutions that I came up with and add ideas of his own. In time, I found that I needed to go to him less often, not because there were fewer problems, but because I was learning to think solutions through for myself.

Although it felt like a difficult lesson to learn to start with – initially I felt unsupported and I just wanted help – his leadership style of thinking through solutions has stuck with me. Now that I am an Assistant Headteacher, I need to consider ways of managing situations quickly. Developing my thinking skills in this way from early on in my career made it easier to transition into leadership.

When you have problems at school, it is important to go to members of the senior leadership team for support. But it is helpful for you and for the leadership team if you have considered the options first. It is easy to respond to situations that take us out of our comfort zone by immediately seeking help from someone else. Often, it is good to sit with a situation for a short while, as your brain will automatically try to problem-solve. Depending on the situation, this is what we would suggest to pupils when they are feeling stuck. It can also be beneficial to talk through a situation with a colleague and discuss different responses or solutions.

By sitting with situations yourself for a brief time, to feel calmer and to problem-solve, before speaking to colleagues, you will develop your own ability to find solutions. As I mentioned earlier, senior leaders and headteachers do not have magic wands to find solutions, but over time they have learned to develop their critical-thinking skills and they have had more experience responding to situations. Draw on their experience only after giving yourself time and space to think about solutions.

Often there is not just one answer or solution, there are different ways forward and it is a case of deciding which option would work best for everyone involved. Sometimes the solution that is chosen will not be popular with everyone and you'll need to empathize with how others feel about the decision.

## THINGS TO PONDER

- What problems might you need to talk to a senior leader about?

- When might you be able to think of your own solutions first, before speaking to someone?

## Challenging Behaviour

Few things play on a teacher's mind or drain them more than high-level challenging behaviour. Children with complex behaviour patterns can test you to the maximum as you try to find strategies that help them to engage. The accumulation of defiant, controlling or disrespectful behaviour by individual pupils can take its toll on a teacher's patience and affect the ethos of the class and the learning environment for other pupils. It is important to recognize how dealing with challenging behaviour can make us feel and how vital it is to consider our self-care when dealing with these situations.

The first thing to consider with challenging behaviour is the reason why the child may be behaving in this way. If we know the underlying reason for the behaviour it is easier to understand, and we are less likely to blame ourselves or take it personally. Has something happened in the child's life that makes them feel unsafe, unloved or on edge? It helps if you know about family situations or changes in circumstances.

Children often need to process events and circumstances that adults would struggle to comprehend. They may feel insecure or unsafe and the behaviour you see is a result of these feelings. The child may not comprehend what is happening to them or the people they love, but they know that something is not right. They may recall moments in the past when they knew something wasn't good in their lives. When children feel unsettled, there will often be a change in their behaviour. It may be a slight change, such as becoming quieter or upset a little more easily than usual. Or it could be that their behaviour is angry, aggressive or dismissive of others.

When a child's behaviour changes, it often rings an alarm bell that something has changed for that child. It may not be something they understand or can express to anyone, but it shows up as a behaviour change. When you try to speak to the child about how they are, they might not want to talk, or they might not be able to express what caused their behaviour.

When you are supporting children presenting with challenging behaviour it is important for you to talk to colleagues. Conversations with colleagues can help us explore our own feelings about the child's behaviour and think about ways to support everyone involved, as well as understanding the child's perspective. It may be helpful to speak to colleagues who have taught the child or their siblings to see if they have behaved like this in the past. Conversations allow you to express your frustrations or concerns with the situation and colleagues may offer advice and support. Also, speak to the senior leadership team so you have support and they are aware of the pupil's behaviour.

When you are dealing with challenging behaviour, it is important to look after your own wellbeing. When you are well, you are likely to find it easier to deal with challenging behaviour and to respond to situations in the best way possible. If you are experiencing a challenging time with behaviour issues, it can take over your thoughts, and you may find yourself thinking about and running through in your mind everything that happened during the day.

You may start questioning your responses. What if you had done something differently? What if something else had not happened that day? Could you have helped the situation? These kinds of questions go around in our minds, searching for answers. Sometimes, we know we could have responded in a different way or someone else in the situation could have responded differently, and that may have helped. Also, the responses may not have made any difference at all. Sometimes children need to work through how they are feeling, and whatever someone else did or did not do would not make much difference. It is worth bearing in mind that once the situation is over, you cannot change the outcome. The only thing you have some control over is when you are able to let the situation go, to stop overthinking it and consider if there is anything you would like to try another time.

If I have had a particularly difficult day dealing with behaviour issues at school, then sometimes I feel extremely tired when I get home – I know I have used lots of energy trying to manage a situation. I find that I may be less reasonable with my family on these days. Even if I go to bed early, I often wake in the night after my mind has tried to process what is going on. When this happens, I know I need to step up my self-care and think about ways to look after myself for my own wellbeing, but also for the benefit of those around me.

There are likely to be times in your career when you need support while dealing with a child with complex behaviour issues. I think that admitting you need support with an individual or a situation shows that you have a good awareness of your own and the child's needs. Sometimes another adult may offer a different perspective on the child's behaviour and this may give you the opportunity to see other strategies. In more challenging circumstances, it may need a team of staff working together to help a distressed child.

When you walk into a difficult situation or have been asked to help with challenging behaviour, such as a child who is being physical, so they are a danger to themselves or others in the environment, it can raise your own stress levels. As I approach these situations, I find it useful to take some deep breaths and try to remain as calm as possible, because the calmer you are the better the child is likely to respond. It is helpful to take the lead from the staff already there. Do they need support managing the upset child? Do they need help managing the rest of the class while they speak to and calm the child who is unsettled?

After working with challenging behaviour, where a child has put themselves or others at risk, it is important to take time to process what has happened. Take some deep breaths, maybe have a drink of water and talk with colleagues about it. If you need to go straight back to teaching, allow yourself time to process the event after you finish that lesson.

## THINGS TO PONDER

- Do you teach children who may present challenging behaviour?

- What strategies have you tried that have been successful in the past?

- Who can you speak to in the school about students' challenging behaviour?

- What can you do to ensure your own self-care?

# Monitoring

Monitoring is part of the teaching cycle and provides schools with a way of self-assessing the learning and progress that is happening in a school. Monitoring can take the form of three teachers working together in a triad, peer-to-peer collaboration with teachers planning or completing a supportive practice together, lesson observations, listening to the opinions of pupils, workbook scrutiny, learning walks, climate walks, drop-in sessions, professional dialogue meetings and many other methods. Class teachers may feel that the monitoring cycle is a judgement. When someone comes into your lesson to observe, you know that your teaching is being scrutinized. It can make you feel nervous, on edge and then overthink everything. However supportive your senior management team is, the process may feel like you are being judged and tested.

The feedback you receive from monitoring should be designed to celebrate what is going well and include suggestions for even-better practice. In the best-case scenarios, this feedback will be a face-to-face experience with an opportunity to have an honest dialogue. It is easy for us to forget all the positive things that have been shared, even if they are numerous, and only focus on the area for development. Our minds have a negative bias and they home in on the negative, so those words stick like glue. We are much more likely to focus on the one or two points for improvement than many points of praise. If we are consciously aware that this is what our minds are likely to do then we can choose to emphasize the positives more – maybe tell someone else about them, write them down or read through them if they are in written format; anything that helps your mind absorb the positives.

As the class teacher, you know your pupils better than anyone else in the school; you understand when a pupil has had a challenging morning before coming to school or if they are struggling for numerous reasons. When you are observed, try to be confident in sharing why certain behaviours occurred or why you chose to use some adult deployment at a certain time. All feedback should be a professional dialogue.

In my school, we are experimenting with monitoring where only positive feedback is given. We started with pupil voice – asking a group of children from each class what they thought was great about their teacher, what they wanted to celebrate. It was a powerful piece of monitoring. Each group only needed to spend about 15 minutes talking for the person monitoring to get a wide range of positive and powerful comments from the children. The impact on staff was incredible.

My Headteacher took a group of children from my class and asked them what they wanted to celebrate about me as a teacher. When the Headteacher told me what the children had said, I felt pride and a huge sense of achievement. What I found particularly powerful was how the positive comments stayed with me, and how I was able to recall many of them several days later. I reflected on why this was the case and I believe it was because my negative bias had nothing to cling on to, as all the comments were positive.

We are going to experiment further to see the impact on staff if they receive only positive feedback. Does it make staff feel more self-assured and confident in their practice? Does it help staff to know that the leadership team believes in them and what they are capable of doing? Does it help staff strive for better results without the development comments?

Peer-to-peer and triad collaborations for aiding teacher development can be a supportive way to enhance everyone's practice. Having a school culture where people are popping in and out of lessons as a general practice can help to reduce anxiety. Heads of departments in secondary, middle and high schools need to know the strengths and areas for development of their departments. In smaller schools, senior leadership teams need this awareness to know how to support everyone in their professional development.

## THINGS TO PONDER

- How do you feel before a monitoring exercise in school?

- What feedback do you remember?

- What would help you to focus on the positive feedback?

# The Joy of Smiling

When we smile, we release endorphins that make us feel better. The amazing thing is that when we smile, we have an impact on those around us too – we help them to feel happier as well. We can create a ripple effect: When we feel happy, we will smile more and make others feel happier, too.

When you are busy in school it can be easy to rush from one thing to the next with your head down, walking past people and not making eye contact. However, if you slow your speed a bit, keep your head up and smile at people you will feel better and calmer. Then you are likely to be more productive in school, as well as helping others feel better for receiving your smile.

When we come in to work in the morning, our heads may be swimming with all the things we need to get done. We may have been creating a mental list of jobs on our journey to school. When we get preoccupied with our mental lists, we can be so involved in what is going on in our heads that we forget to be polite and courteous to our colleagues. By smiling and saying 'good morning' we are making connections with people we work alongside. Connections are important in teaching because although we have lots of human contact throughout the day, we don't have much adult contact and that can feel quite isolating.

When you consciously decide to smile more you decrease your stress levels and feel more connected to those around you, which has a positive effect on your mood. Research has proved that smiling is good for your immune system too, because your body produces more white blood cells when you smile and this helps you to fight off illness.[1] Smiling makes you appear more approachable, so your interactions are likely to be easier – when we release endorphins, we also feel calmer.

Smiling is also useful if you need to speak with a parent. If you approach the parent smiling, then you will feel calmer going into the conversation and it is likely that they will be more neutral when you speak to them. Smiling is contagious and our brain responds to someone smiling at us by smiling back. When greeting a parent, you can help to put them more at ease by smiling.

When I first started teaching there was a saying about teachers not smiling until Christmas, as a way of implementing strong behaviour management in class. I never agreed with that school of thought – how could being straight-faced and grumpy help a child to feel welcomed and settled in a class? The more we smile when we greet our pupils and throughout our classes, the calmer and more settled everyone is likely to be.

Noticing someone in a positive way is a great way to connect with them; it helps them feel recognized. My school completed a whole-school project called Positive Noticing Day, where every person in the school wrote positive comments about others. The teachers identified something positive about each individual pupil in their class on a parcel tag, onto which the other pupils added more positive comments. The children then wore the parcel tags on their clothes proudly and with huge smiles, knowing they were recognized and appreciated. In addition, our Headteacher wrote a positive comment parcel tag for every child and member of staff in the school. The project was part of a larger event inspired by the work of Paul Dix, in which 600 schools participated.[2] The positive noticing took about half an hour of lesson time, as well as teacher time to write positive tags, but the impact was massive; many children chose to wear their parcel tags for days after the event or used them as bookmarks. The positive noticing created a culture of happiness, with every person feeling valued for being themselves.

## A Sense of Humour

I think being able to laugh and enjoy your job makes teaching feel even more rewarding. We are privileged to be able to work with some of the best comedians – children! Most days, if not multiple times a day, a child says or does something that brings a smile to my face. When you work with younger children their innocence and wonder about the world can often be amusing. My husband recalls many funny tales about students in his secondary school as well.

Some of the funny tales that I can recall were the smallest of incidents, but they have left an impression. Some years ago, I had given a class a story starter: Hector was an incredible hamster. The children discussed ideas with each other about how Hector might have been incredible – what things he might have done. When the children began writing their stories, I moved around the room to see how they were getting on. One child was sitting with their pencil on the table and they were looking around the room. I asked if they needed help but they replied that they had finished. I looked at their book to see just one line: Hector was an incredible hamster until he died! What a great sense of humour that child had.

In another class, there was a child who was funny and cheeky. He loved to be active and have fun but did not like writing. One day we were doing some writing and when I scanned around the room everyone seemed to be on task. On closer inspection, this child had not written anything, even though it appeared that he was writing. I asked him where his work was, and he replied that he had used his invisible pen that day so I might not be able to see his great writing! He proceeded to tell me some of the ideas he had written with his invisible pen.

Bringing humour into your day helps to lighten the atmosphere in your classroom, helping to make it a more relaxed environment for the children to learn in and for you to teach in. Sharing humorous tales with colleagues in the staffroom can help lift the spirits of those around you and often encourages others to share their funny anecdotes. Sometimes we can take everything too seriously and a bit of humour helps to raise happiness levels.

One story that is often retold in our staffroom happened a while back when a class was learning about Joseph and his amazing coloured coat. The class teacher had bought a black coat from a charity shop for the children to create their own coloured dream coat. They left the coat in the staffroom, so a teaching assistant went to fetch it for the lesson. The class was fully immersed in decorating and transforming the coat when one of the children tried it on for everyone to see what they had created so far. When they put their hands in the coat pockets, they found they were full of personal belongings. The wrong coat had been collected from the staffroom and a member of staff's winter coat had been fully decorated! Luckily the staff member had a great sense of humour, though the class teacher was mortified by what had happened.

Often you need to have a sense of humour when you are tackling sex education as part of the curriculum. One day, when teaching young children the correct name for body parts, we drew outlines of chalk bodies on the playground and labelled body parts using the vocabulary we had learned in the lesson. Near the end of the lesson, when discussing male body parts, one child started to talk about peanuts and tentacles instead of penis and testicles! It was one of those moments when you need to keep a straight face so the child is not embarrassed; you need to gently correct them and then laugh about it later.

When I was teaching older primary pupils who were learning about changes to their bodies, I asked if they had any questions. One child asked why they sell flavoured condoms. I saw my teaching assistant's shoulders start to tremble as she tried to contain a giggle and I had to think quickly. The children were too young to know the real reason, so I said it had to do with advertising – to make them more attractive for people to want to use them and easier for them to sell! I still work with that teaching assistant, and she still laughs out loud when she recalls that story.

## THINGS TO PONDER

- What funny incidents, stories or events have happened to you recently? It could be tiny things that brought a smile to your face.
- Who in your staffroom lifts the mood with amusing anecdotes?

# Teaching Wins

Many people go into teaching because they want to make a difference – they want to have a positive impact on young people's lives. In all honesty, every teacher has the ability to make a difference to children each day, but most of the time it is a subtle difference that is hard to quantify or recognize. Most shifts are small, but lots of the small shifts lead to big changes. By being positive, consistent and reliable you will make a difference to the children you teach. It is important to take time to reflect on the differences that have been created. If you are fortunate enough to work with a teaching assistant or in a team, it is great to do this together. It may be that you notice that the levels of concentration and resilience have improved for individuals or a whole class. You may have noticed an improvement in the quality of a pupil's use of vocabulary or confidence in using a method to solve a Maths problem. Try celebrating the differences you have noticed.

Sometimes you have a huge teaching win. One of my friends who teaches secondary pupils told me about a class she had been struggling with that had a high level of need. One child in her class was a selective mute and had poor attendance. At a parents' evening, she spoke to the child's parents about her concerns regarding attendance and tried to engage the pupil in the discussion. In the weeks that followed, there was a significant improvement in this child's attendance. One day, when the class was taking turns to share their work, the child put her hand up to share what she had written; the rest of the class was respectful while she read out her work. My friend was so proud of her and the environment that she, as her teacher, had created to enable this pupil to have the courage to speak up. Since that time, the child continued to grow in confidence and quietly shared her ideas and work in the class. These big teaching wins do not happen all the time and when they do they need to be celebrated. Sharing accounts like this with your colleagues helps to raise everyone's morale and sense of hope.

Once, I taught a child who was anxious about leaving his parents each morning. He would get upset when his parents handed him over to me each day. After a few minutes he usually calmed down and was fine for the remainder of the day, but it was the initial separation that he found traumatic. I collaborated with his parents to form a plan, as it was distressing for them too, leaving him upset each day and not being sure when he would settle. We started with his parents drawing a small heart on their son's arm so that he could press it and send his parents love whenever he wished. His parents also drew small hearts on their wrists so they could send him love too. He found this reassuring. His dad then devised a plan to gradually, at his son's pace, say goodbye one step nearer the gate each day, leaving the child to walk an extra step on their own towards the class line in the playground. The child felt comfortable with this plan because it progressed at their pace. When he trusted the system, that his parents would gradually move further back, and our staff team would praise him for lining up himself, he hurried the plan along so that he soon left his parents happily at the gate. Collaborating with the parents and noticing the significance of separation anxiety helped the child to have a big win by becoming more independent and confident. As this child became more confident in separating from his parents, we saw a change in his learning in school. He was more willing to share his ideas with the class, he helped his peers more readily and was happier. This teaching win started as something very small – noticing how traumatic a child found the first few minutes of the school day after separating from his parents – but the impact on his learning and self-esteem was huge. Being collaborative and working in partnership with children and their parents is energizing.

The start of every school year is always slightly different as you have a new cohort of children, and you may find yourself in a different teaching space and collaborating with new colleagues. Some classes can come to you with a certain reputation. You have a choice to either heed the reputation or get to know the class and then form your own opinion. Sometimes it is easy to get swept along with negative thoughts or perceptions that can then reinforce that reputation. If we look at things with fresh eyes, we may find a different perspective.

The new school year is also a fresh start for the pupils we teach, a chance for them to express their true selves. By establishing clear expectations for the class, and by being consistent, I have found the children get used to how I work and often any previous reputations fade away. Sometimes the small choices we make can affect our thinking and approach to a situation.

No matter how small the teaching win is, it is worth recognizing and celebrating. These small wins help us to reaffirm that what we do makes a difference. Our small wins add up to make differences in the lives of the children we teach. They also help us to recognize that we are doing a good job. Sometimes we keep working but we question the impact we are having. By recognizing our teaching wins, we can stop doubting and believe in the difference we make.

## THINGS TO PONDER

- What teaching wins have you experienced recently?

- Who is a good person to share your wins with?

- How many small wins can you remember?

- What small changes will help you or the pupils you teach?

# Feeling Under Threat

In our school, we have practice drills for fire alarms and lockdown situations. Across the world there will be practice drills for different reasons, such as tornadoes or other extreme weather conditions. There may be drills for bomb threats, shootings in the area or other extreme emergencies. Different schools and areas will have different systems, procedures and regulations, but the aim for all schools will be to practise what to do so that everyone knows the drill, and everyone can stay calm in an emergency. It is important to share with senior staff anything you notice that doesn't work during a drill so that the situation can be thought through for another occasion.

One of my friends was the Headteacher of an international school in Texas, USA, and he described how he felt constantly under threat from attacks. On several occasions, shootings and gunshots were reported in the local area leading to a campus lockdown. His school had security on campus day and night. They had consultancy firms who would test to see if they could breach the school's security system. They even built a new glass building with a distanced perimeter fence, because they were told the glass would allow them to see any threat coming and the open ground would give them time to lock down the building with a touch of a button.

In Texas it is common for people to carry guns, but his school forbade any guns on school premises until recently. One day a Texas sheriff went to the school to watch his son play football. He was wearing his uniform, including a gun in a holster. The parents at the school were not happy that someone had a gun on campus, so my friend spoke to the sheriff who explained that he had to carry a gun by law in Texas and usually people were comforted by him being there.

Schools have procedures and policies in place to keep everyone safe but sometimes these procedures need adapting and improving. It is important to let senior staff know if you notice things that may need to change. When you are dealing with stressful situations, you are holding the pupils that you support as well as dealing with your own emotions. If possible, take time after an event to check in with yourself and see what you need. If you are struggling then please find someone to speak to.

# CHAPTER 3

# Basic Self-Care

*'Aim to make a difference in someone's life
every single day, including your own.'*

DOE ZANTAMATA

What is self-care? What are the benefits? Teaching is time-pressured and when we are tired it is easy to neglect ourselves. Prioritizing our self-care and making time for ourselves for just 10 minutes a day can impact our outlook and how we feel. Even slight changes to our routine may have a positive influence on our wellbeing. In this chapter, I share tools and strategies that are easily implemented and may offer noticeable benefits. I will explain how these techniques have helped my own self-care and led to me being able to support the wellbeing of those around me.

In the coming pages, I will invite you to audit different aspects of your life and how you are feeling so that you can build or adapt your own self-care routine.

# What Is Self-Care?

Self-care sounds self-explanatory – we just need to look after ourselves. I find that I have good intentions for self-care but in practice it takes a bit of work. In teaching there is always a never-ending list of things that you could do to make your classroom and teaching the absolute best that they can be, but if you tried to do it all you would burn out.

I've found some of the best methods of self-care are the simplest ones that I can include in my day without feeling like they are more tasks to do. When life is already busy, just pausing and taking time for yourself can feel impossible. We need to find ways to make time for ourselves without feeling like it is a burden or too much effort. We need to know that we will feel better after doing something for ourselves and that there are real benefits to making time for our wellbeing.

Constantly neglecting our own needs can have a detrimental effect on our lives. If we keep pushing on and putting everyone else's needs first and thinking about ourselves last, we can become resentful. Prioritizing ourselves even for 10 minutes a day can have an enormous impact on our outlook and how we feel. Having a small amount of time dedicated to something just for yourself can feel indulgent at first, but in time I've come to realize I'm nicer to be around when I take that short amount of time.

Sometimes it can be hard to know where to start – how to make time for yourself. Consider beginning with small things, such as having a peaceful bath or shower. Or you may take five minutes to stop and have a cup of tea without doing anything else at the same time. You may decide to put on your favourite song and just listen to it or dance around singing at the top of your voice. You might go to a quiet space to read a chapter of a book undisturbed. These are all simple acts of self-care, but they are effective, especially if you make a conscious decision to do them. Consider if any of these small acts of self-care are things you would choose to do, or if you have thought of something you would prefer instead.

## SIMPLE ACTS OF SELF-CARE

Let us start by thinking about what it feels like when you look after yourself. Answer these questions honestly and you will start to produce simple ideas for your self-care. You may choose to consider answers in your head or journal your responses by writing them down.

- What is your favourite thing you do to look after yourself?

- When do you most need to practise self-care?

- What happens when you neglect self-care?

- What one thing could you do today that feels like self-care?

# The Importance of Sleep

Simple self-care strategies usually include thinking about sleep. We all need sleep to function and be our best selves. When we have several nights of disturbed sleep it can have an adverse impact on how we perceive situations, our performance and energy levels. We all know that sleep is important, but we do not always prioritize it. So, what can we do? Firstly, just being aware of your sleep patterns can make a difference.

# YOUR SLEEP PATTERNS

Think about the following questions to help you become aware of your current sleep situation.

- Are you conscious of the time you go to bed?

- How easy do you find it getting to sleep?

- Are you able to stay asleep during the night?

- Do you wake at a regular time?

- Are there times when you find it harder to sleep?

Once we have an awareness about a situation, even if it is not what we would like it to be, then we can start thinking about how we can improve it. It may be that you notice that you fall asleep quickly but that you wake in the middle of the night or early in the morning. The good news is that whatever is happening, there are small things you can do to help you feel more in control of your sleep routine.

If you have noticed that you have trouble getting to sleep, then you may want to consider what your evening routine looks like. I find that if I am working late into the evening, it can be harder to switch off and I start to overthink things. If possible, I try not to work past a certain point in the evening. There have been many research studies into watching screens before bedtime and the negative effect this can have on sleep patterns.

Having a wind-down routine can help you to get to sleep more easily. Decide on a time when you are going to finish work each day; this may vary depending on your commitments each day, but try to stick to this time. Think about the small things that help you to relax; it may be taking a bath or shower, listening to a podcast or meditation, sitting down to read, watching TV or phoning a friend. I find it useful to journal before I go to sleep – I write a short paragraph about the day, noting things that have happened, how I have felt or any thoughts I had. Journalling helps me to park anything from the day that may be niggling or to celebrate something that I'm happy about.

Thinking about three things that you are grateful for is a good exercise to help you release happy hormones and make it easier to get to sleep. These three things can be as big or small as you like. You might include a moment when someone smiled at you, asked how you were or held the door for you. Maybe you are grateful for a cosy bed, a caring friend, or a healthy family member. You may be grateful for the same things each day, or you could challenge yourself to think about different things each day. You can think about your three items of gratitude, write them down or share them with someone else.

Recently, I attended a course run by a training company, The Art of Brilliance, and learned about an alphabet of gratitude, where you think about something that you are grateful for starting with each letter of the alphabet. I find this technique useful if I wake up in the night and my mind starts focusing on unnecessary thoughts when I want to get back to sleep. If you find that you get to sleep but then wake in the night and struggle to get back to sleep, then consciously doing something to quieten your mind and relax your body can help. An alternative idea to an alphabet of gratitude could be writing down all the things that are going through your mind so you do not have to worry about them and can hopefully go back to sleep – this is harder if you share a room with someone else.

You may like to try listening to a meditation track or following a mindfulness activity. There are several mindfulness activities later in this book, but one that is good for sleep is imagining that you are breathing in and out through your feet – breathing in from the soles of your feet, with the breath travelling up and all through your body, then breathing out, imagining the breath going down and out of your feet. Although this activity may sound strange, it helps to transfer your attention from your thoughts to your feet. You are also likely to take longer, slower breaths as you breathe in and out, imagining the breath travelling around your body, so your breathing will slow down, and your body and mind can settle.

A wonderful time to practise gratitude is as soon as you wake up in the morning; try saying to yourself three things that you are grateful for, to make a positive start to your day. Teachers often wake up thinking about all the things they need to do before the class they teach arrives that morning, which is an overwhelming way to start the day. Thinking about what you are grateful for is a kinder way to start.

## Staying Hydrated

Drinking enough water is a basic need that is easy to forget when you are having a busy day. Many teachers use their breaktime to set up and prepare for the next lesson. You may rush to use the toilet, which inevitably has a long queue with everyone having the same brief time slot. I often find that I have rushed to the toilet but have forgotten to take my water bottle to fill up and then I run out of time to collect it.

We need to prioritize hydrating ourselves in order to do our job in the best possible way. Without hydration, we do not function to the best of our ability. Our cognitive functioning slows down, making it harder for us to process information. If we are not hydrated, we are far more likely to end the day with a headache, as well as feeling more exhausted because the body is having to work harder to maintain itself.

Some teachers worry that if they drink to stay hydrated, then they will need to go to the bathroom more frequently. I hope that most schools now have a culture where it is always okay for an adult to go to the bathroom when they need to – again this is a basic human need. I understand that to do this depends on the adult support in the classroom or the close support of a nearby class teacher. It is a conversation worth having in school so that adults are not restricting their consumption of water due to fear of needing the bathroom.

## Exercise and Nutrition

We all know the benefits of exercise for developing strong muscles, supporting your bones and helping your heart health. For us as teachers, equally important benefits of exercise include the release of endorphins to help us feel happier, doing something for ourselves and the chance of better sleep. Exercise is something that may be just for you. When you teach, it is easy to feel that you support and nurture others all the time and that you prioritize yourself last. Many people come into teaching because they have a caring, thoughtful nature and they naturally think about others before themselves. However, it is important to do things for yourself so that you can continue to support others. Finding a form of exercise that makes you feel good and that you enjoy is vital. You do not want exercise to become another item on your list of things to do. When you have found something that you enjoy and look forward to doing, see if you can make a regular slot in your week to include it.

When my children were younger, they both went to karate and at their first session the instructor asked if I wanted to join in. I had previously done karate in my teens so agreed to try a session. It was a success and for several years, all three of us attended karate sessions together – it was a fantastic way to spend quality time with my family. All of us had a shared interest and known group of friends, whilst having a purposeful way to exercise. It was the easiest way to ensure I was exercising as well as being with my children. I benefitted physically and mentally from these twice-weekly karate sessions. When you do any sort of martial art you cannot focus on anything else. If I had experienced a challenging day at work, I would not be able to think about what happened whilst I was training. I found karate was an effective way to release tension from my body. It is important to find something that you like doing, exercise that you enjoy and look forward to doing.

Alongside exercise, nutrition is another important factor while teaching. Choosing a nutritious breakfast is key, because unexpected incidents can happen in school and your lunch break may be shortened while you deal with something. I find it useful to batch cook and freeze lunches; that way I know I have a healthy, filling lunch each day. As I said in Chapter 1, my husband and I also batch cook dinners for the freezer to ensure that we have a bank of meals ready for busy term-time weeks. Eating nutritious food daily will help you to feel better in yourself.

# When We Are Ill

Teachers are constantly exposed to whatever germs the children in the classroom have. I teach younger children who still want to hold your hand but who don't always have the best hygiene. This can make us susceptible to picking up different illnesses from our environment. If you add the fact that our immune system weakens the more tired we get, it is not surprising that many educators limp to the end of term or become unwell. When you are ill, I think it can be hard to know if you should go to work, as you may feel guilty if you stay at home. Most schools are so tightly staffed that you know your absence puts more strain on the rest of the team. It can be difficult to decide whether to go to work, knowing you need to be firing on all cylinders to do the job well, or take a day off as your body is telling you that you need to rest.

I have known members of staff who come into school when they are so poorly that, as part of the senior leadership team, I have asked them if they should be there. Are they well enough to be in school, as health and family always come first? It's hard to ask people this, as I understand how they are feeling and know the dilemma they are facing. They do not want to let anyone down; however, without rest they cannot get better. It is much easier to advise someone else about what they should do than decide what to do when you are ill. When you need to decide for yourself then self-doubt creeps in about whether you are ill enough to need a day off.

When we are not feeling our best but decide to go to school, then we need to take care of ourselves. We need to let the people we work with know that we are not feeling our best. We need to think about how we teach that day and be as kind to ourselves as possible. When I am unwell, I find it is much easier if I stick to a routine as the children know what to expect and their behaviour is often better. Sticking to a routine also helps me as I know what I am doing and what resources need to be prepared. The children know when we are not well, and it may make them feel less settled in class. This is where the familiarity of routine helps them feel safer too.

When you are not feeling your best but choose to work, I think it is a good idea to think about what is coming up in the curriculum that is an easier lesson, one that doesn't require many resources or that you know the children will be fully immersed in during independent working. These types of activities in your curriculum are ideal for days when you are not on top form. Also, be kind to yourself with marking on days when you are not feeling great. While the pupils are working, circulate around the class to give immediate feedback but do not labour marking. After work on these days, aim to leave as soon as you can to allow your body to rest and recover. If all these suggestions don't make a difference, then you may need to question whether you were well enough to be teaching in school.

There have been times, several years ago, when I have been on the verge of burnout – when I ignored the warning signals that my body sent me. One time I remember vividly was when I was trying to change a display in my classroom. I took down the border and backing paper only to put the same border and paper back up – twice! My mind was so overloaded that I was not present with what I was doing, and I was making many mistakes. What worries me now thinking back to that time is how present was I when teaching my class? How present was I with my own children at home? I became quite ill with bronchitis, needing strong antibiotics and an inhaler. My whole body and mind were exhausted and overwhelmed resulting in me not functioning well anywhere and feeling awful. This episode scared me into wanting to make a change, so it would not happen again. It was soon after this incident that I discovered tapping and I became more disciplined with my mindfulness practices.

## Learning to Say NO!

Self-care sometimes means knowing when you need to say no, when you are coping with too much already and your plate is full. An analogy that is useful to bear in mind is a table loaded with coins. Each coin represents things that need to be done, things that need some thought, decisions that need to be made and people that we support. These coins can pile up and the more they pile up the more pressure we feel.

We don't have any control over some of the coins on the table, but we do over others. Some coins represent things we are expected to do, we may feel it is our duty or our obligation to do, or something else. They can be things that we have always done so we feel we should continue with them. It could be that you feel like you would be letting others down without doing an act of service. Other coins may represent something that you enjoy, but you feel like you must shoehorn it in to be able to do it.

The more coins that are added, the more pressure the table (you) feels until one day one of the legs gives way and many of the coins fall. At this point we feel like we have failed, that we should have been able to keep adding more and continuing to cope. We feel like not only have we let ourselves down, but we have also let down those around us. We may start to worry about what others will think about us and become consumed by negative self-doubts.

The challenge is recognizing when you are reaching your limit, when things are getting too much, and taking action. I find when I get to this point some things start to change in my life. Often when I am reaching my limit, I get very tired and need to go to bed much earlier than usual. I find I wake in the night with worries. My exercise routine drops out as I don't feel that I have the energy or time to do it, even though I know I would feel better for doing it. I stop eating as healthily as I would like as my body craves chocolate and sugar, because it seeks energy. Some of these things may sound familiar to you and this may happen when you are reaching your limit, or you may recognize different things in yourself.

I have found that if I ignore warning signs in my body then I become more emotional, have a shorter temper and become physically ill. On one occasion this led to burnout. I would not want that to happen to anyone and I work hard to prevent it from happening to me again.

When I feel like I am reaching my limit I make myself stop and take stock. I write down anything that feels overwhelming or anything that is not working – at home or school. I write down what is going well too – I think it is important to recognize the positives as well. Once I have written down everything, I then consider what I can change. I think about what small things I can do that might make a difference. I then think about the things that I need to say no to. What coins do I have on my table that I need to acknowledge I cannot do? Which is one coin too many? If I feel like I am going to be letting people down by saying no to something, I find it useful to write a letter to them – one that I will never post. This acts as a way of getting thoughts clear in my head about what I would like to say. Sometimes writing the letter and not sending it is enough. Other times, having written the letter, I feel I can have a more coherent conversation without feeling like I am blurting out all the thoughts in my head in a random order.

When you recognize that you are having physical, psychological or emotional warning signs that things are getting too much, you need to start saying no! As we have already said, there is always so much on a teacher's to-do list and then more things are always added by ourselves and others. We need to consider which things on our lists we need to do because they will benefit us, our students or the school. We also need to consider if there are items that don't benefit us or the students we teach – these are the ones to say no to, if we have any. These items should be moved to the bottom of the list for a later date or struck from the list if they have no worth.

Sometimes we must have difficult conversations when we are asked to do something that we don't have the capacity to do and we need to say that we are unable to help. These conversations can feel especially difficult if you usually do as you are asked. If you don't like confrontation and you are worried about saying you can't do something, then you may find yourself defending your decision. I can be like this; I can overthink a situation and worry about what the other person might think of me. Sometimes I have imaginary conversations in my head about how they will react. When you are honest and say you just cannot do something, I've found people respect your honesty and recognize that you would have made a considered choice. I am not suggesting you say no to everything or that you are aggressive in the way you say it. There is a way to say no without being confrontational.

I think before you agree or disagree to do something, give yourself time to think about it. Don't feel like you have to give an answer straight away to someone when you are asked to do something, unless it needs immediate attention. For example, if you are asked whether you would like to attend a course, reply that you would like some time to think about it first. By giving yourself some thinking time, you give yourself space to make a considered decision about whether it is something you would like to do and if you have the capacity to do it. It helps you to feel like you have some control over what you are adding to your plate.

Your leadership team should appreciate that you are making considered decisions and respect what you have decided. If you say no to something it can feel like you may be judged by the person who has asked you; this is our negative bias kicking in. It is very unlikely that anyone is going to judge you for making a considered decision. However, your brain cannot help but look for the negative in a situation, to worry and put you on alert. If you know that you have decided what is best for yourself, then this negative bias should be fleeting. It is your way of self-regulating, to check you have made a decision that is right for you.

If you are trying to decide and you really don't know what the best choice would be, consider the advantages and disadvantages.

This does not need to be a long process. Can you think of three advantages to doing something and three disadvantages? Whichever is the stronger list is probably your best choice. The more you practise doing this the quicker your decision-making process becomes and you are more secure in your judgement – you doubt yourself less.

## THINGS TO PONDER

-   What happens when you are reaching your limit?

-   How good are you at recognizing that you're near your limit?

-   What would it feel like to say no?

-   What are the advantages and disadvantages of agreeing to do more?

## BRINGING JOY

You may like to try this task to discover how to nurture yourself and know that you are doing things to support your wellbeing each day. Start by writing a list of as many things as you can think of that bring you joy. At the top of your list write, 'The things that bring me joy are...'. Then give yourself seven minutes to write as many things as you can that bring you joy. If you feel stuck for ideas, try writing the phrase 'The things that bring me joy' again. Then see if any more ideas come to you. Some ideas could be playing a musical instrument, singing in the shower, stroking your cat's belly, the feel of your feet crunching on ice, the smell of washing that has been dried outside or the taste of ice cream on a hot day. Be imaginative. It might help you to think about your senses - what do you enjoy tasting, smelling, seeing, feeling and hearing? I would add to that, what do you enjoy experiencing? You may get to the end of the seven minutes and still have more ideas, just keep writing them down.

Once you have your list, go through it and mark the things that bring you joy that you could do this week. Have another look at your list and mark in a separate way any of the things you could experience today. When could you do them today? Have you already achieved anything today that is on your list?

. . . . . . . . . . . . . . . . . . . . . . .

## Having a Choice

Sometimes when we are busy, and there is so much to do, we forget that we have a choice. We can choose what we want to spend our time doing. We can choose to do what fills us with joy and nourishment; we can choose to do what we know will make the biggest difference. When we recognize and remember that we have a choice our perspective shifts. We feel more in control and know that we are in charge of creating our own lives.

There will always be things that we need to do, but often we can choose when we do them. When the things you need to do are not inspiring, it is worth considering how they can be completed with the minimal impact. Can you sandwich them between things that you enjoy, so there is an incentive to get them completed as efficiently and quickly as possible without having a negative impact on you?

We have choices about how we spend our leisure time too. Sometimes we feel too tired to make choices, and then spending hours scrolling on the phone or watching TV feel like the easiest options. Try writing a list of things that you enjoy and find relaxing and try doing some of these instead.

## YOUR SELF-CARE BOOSTERS

To help you consider what things in your day or in your life boost you and make you feel better about yourself, try this writing task. Write a list titled: 'Things that boost me'. Give yourself seven minutes to write what gives you a daily boost and makes you feel good about yourself. It may be things like eating a healthy breakfast, reading a book, walking the dog, seeing a friend, going for a run, a fitness class, a good sleep or leaving work before 5 p.m. You may find that the things that boost you were also on your list of things that bring you joy – that is okay. Sometimes rephrasing the statement helps you think of different ideas. Keep writing until the time has run out. You may get to the end of your seven minutes and still have more ideas – give yourself permission to keep writing them down. You may find that your ideas are drying up after a few minutes. If this happens try writing the phrase 'Things that boost me' a few times and see if more ideas come. Sometimes we need to give our minds time to think more deeply.

Once you have your list of things that boost you, I invite you to complete the table on page 72. The bottom row is for things you will aim to do each day, the middle row for things you aim to do each week and the top row is for things you will do when you can. I have included example entries in the table below, but you can write whatever you like in your table.

Example table of nurturing things:

| When I Can | Long walk in the woods | Meet a friend for tea and cake | Family beach walk | A mindfulness retreat |
| --- | --- | --- | --- | --- |
| Each Week | Speak to a friend | A longer meditation | A yoga session | A walk in nature |
| Every Day | Think about something I am grateful for | Practise STOP mindfulness practice *(see page 111)* | Tap for five minutes | Have a bath |

Your table of nurturing things for you:

| When I Can | | | | |
| --- | --- | --- | --- | --- |
| Each Week | | | | |
| Every Day | | | | |

Once you have a list of things that will make you feel better if you do them each day then it becomes easier to make them part of your routine. You might like to tick them off when you have completed them. You may like to change your table every few weeks or have a different one for term time and for during the holidays. It is so easy to be consumed with teaching and daily life that you may feel there is no time for yourself. Building in small things that you have chosen to do each day helps to make things feel more balanced.

. . . . . . . . . . . . . . . . . . . . . . . . .

We can also make a choice about how we want to be when we come home from work or when we speak to friends about our work. I have found it useful to park my day at the front door to enjoy being fully present with my family when I first get home. Then I can enjoy myself with them without my day at school impacting on this time. That does not mean I do not share my day with them, but I think about being my best self for a few minutes when I first get home.

When I park my day before walking into the house, I notice that I do not feel parental guilt for not being present for my children, as I am fully present when I walk through the door. They have my full attention to talk if they wish. As my children have grown older, they now ask how my day has been. I know that this is my opportunity to create a realistic model for my children, to share the funny, good and sometimes challenging things that have happened in my day. This helps them to know work is a balance as they start their first part-time jobs. No one day is completely good or bad – most days have elements of feeling many different ways and that is okay.

It is easier sometimes to focus on the negative, the things that have not gone as you had hoped, especially when you are tired at the end of the day. So consciously deciding to be your best self as you walk through the door can make a huge difference. It changes your mindset and helps you recognize the balance in the day.

## THINGS TO PONDER

- What choices do you intentionally choose to make?

- What can you do to help yourself feel happier?

# When It All Gets Too Much

There will be times when it all feels too much, when you feel like you are working as hard as you possibly can, you are tired and drained, and it still doesn't feel like you are doing enough. I believe that all teachers have probably felt like this at some point – I certainly have! You can feel defeated and exhausted, and you question what you are doing. Know that it is normal to feel like this sometimes, but not all the time. If you are feeling like this regularly, please seek support from someone at school in a leadership position, your doctor or someone you trust.

There have been times when I have been writing this book, when I've had a particularly busy week at home and school, and everything has got on top of me. I have felt like a fraud writing a book to support teachers with their wellbeing when at times my own wellbeing needs attention. I have questioned if it is the right thing to be writing a book about this subject. When this has happened, I have done what I am suggesting you do when you feel like this – I have spoken to people at home and at school that I trust. I have talked through how I am feeling – I have acknowledged the doubts and emotions. I have journalled my thoughts and looked for the areas in life to express gratitude each day. I've continued to tap on what I'm experiencing and I've listened to guided meditations, and these actions have made it easier to manage. In a way, it has also made me recognize the need for books like this – which are honest and realistic. I have tried all the strategies and suggestions in this book, and they all help.

## YOUR ACTION PLAN

I encourage you to try this exercise and consider these questions, so that the next time it all feels too much you have an action plan to support you.

– What warning red flags do you have when things are starting to get on top of you?

– What kinds of thoughts do you have when things are getting too much?

– Who can you talk to when you feel like things are becoming overwhelming?

– What self-care strategies can you put into place that instantly help you feel better? (You may want to refer to your list of things that bring you joy, *see page 69*, and your list of things that boost you, *see page 71*.)

- What self-care strategies can you do each day that will help you become more aware when things are getting too much?

- How can you slow down? What things can you let go?

It may be beneficial to answer these questions at a time when you feel okay and again when things feel too much and compare your answers. If you are answering the questions in a similar way both times, then you are likely to be aware of the warning signals that your body gives you. If your answers are very different, depending on how you are feeling at the time, it may be useful to refer to your answers at times of stress to help you know what's best for you.

. . . . . . . . . . . . . . . . . . . . . . . .

# Community Support

Schools are small communities that all have one common interest – supporting pupils to thrive and learn. When you are struggling, someone in the school community can often help you. Knowing that there is someone you can talk to and who cares can make a huge difference to your ability to cope. When you start at a new school, it is important to know who you can talk to and your rights in the system you are working in. You need to know what you can and cannot do, as well as your legal rights.

Friends of ours went to teach in an international school in Shanghai, China. They did not speak Chinese but discovered a close community of teachers from around the world who were welcoming, friendly and chose to socialize together. The school community became like a family where the staff supported each other. Our friends talk fondly about what they call TIC days – standing for

This Is China. At times when they felt like everything was going wrong – issues with visas or banking or simply being able to get a taxi – or on days when they felt isolated and alone in a country where it was difficult to communicate their needs due to language barriers, if they shared how they were feeling, the community stood up to support them. They did not just send a text expressing sympathy, but they actively showed up asking what they could do to help – from offering childcare to make it easier to visit the bank, to speaking to human resources to help with visas.

It is important for all of us to rely on and support each other. To do this we need to share our vulnerability. Everyone has a bad day and remembers a time when they have needed support. People can only support you if you are willing to share that you are finding things difficult. When we do share our vulnerability, it makes it easier for others to share that they are having a hard time; it offers us an opportunity to pay it forward.

## SELF-CARE TOP TIPS

Remember that when you feel under pressure and need to take care of yourself, try to:

- stay hydrated

- sleep

- think about what small things you can do just for you

- consider what brings you joy

# PART II

# Mindfulness

# CHAPTER 4

# Introduction to Mindfulness

*'Mindfulness means paying attention*
*in a particular way: on purpose, in the*
*present moment and nonjudgementally.'*

JON KABAT-ZINN

What is mindfulness? And what are the benefits of practising mindfulness?

Mindfulness helps us to respond rather than react to situations as we learn to live in the present moment and become more aware of our current circumstances and thoughts. In the following pages, I will equip you with knowledge and understanding about how our bodies react to stress and how we can learn to choose how we respond. I will invite you to notice how you react to different situations and acknowledge how your reaction is influenced by both the initial trigger or event and the following negative self-talk and reprimand. This insight helps us reflect on when we have judged ourselves harshly, so we are aware of this in the future and hopefully choose a kinder way to be – to be nonjudgemental.

# What Is Mindfulness?

Mindfulness is paying attention – it involves paying attention to your thoughts, feelings and anything that is going on around you. That does not mean that you need always to be on high alert or super vigilant to feel that you are being completely present. It is about having a conscious awareness of what you are doing and what you are thinking. When you practise mindfulness, you are more likely to notice if you are being critical about yourself and then you can decide if that is something you want to continue doing. You are more likely to notice how different situations make you feel or react. When you practise mindfulness over time you can choose to respond to situations rather than react.

I have noticed that the longer I practise mindfulness the more aware I am about when things feel too much – it has helped me to know when I need to slow down, take a breath and decide what I want to do or how I want to respond. Sometimes you know in advance when an event is likely to feel overwhelming; for example, if your school is due for an inspection there is a high chance that you will feel under pressure with a desire to do the best that you can for yourself and the school. When you know in advance that you are going into a stressful situation, then being aware of your body and thoughts will help you to pause and give yourself a moment to take stock of your situation.

At other times, our stress levels may peak due to individual circumstances – maybe someone has said something that has brought up a memory from the past, maybe you are dealing with some challenging behaviour, maybe someone very close to you is going through a difficult time and you are concerned about them. When we are coping with higher stress levels, practising mindfulness can help us to take a break and pause, then we often find we can cope a bit more easily. We give our minds and bodies a short break before continuing. When we do this regularly, we help our brain to create new neural pathways.

There is sometimes a perception that to practise mindfulness you need to sit completely still and your mind should be clear. This is not the case; you can be mindful when you are moving and when your mind keeps getting distracted. You can be mindful at any time and in most places – you can be mindful queuing up to pay for your food shopping by simply being present in what you are doing or by paying attention to your breath whilst you wait for the person in front of you to finish. Although there are benefits from doing regular longer practices of mindfulness, there are also benefits from doing small acts regularly throughout your day.

## The Benefits of Mindfulness

There are many well-researched benefits of practising mindfulness. When you practise mindfulness, you are training the brain to pay attention to what you are doing in the present moment and by developing this skill it becomes easier to focus. You are giving yourself time, time to just be, to be aware. By giving yourself time, you provide space for your mind and body to slow down, to process and acknowledge how you are feeling. Often, we are so busy jumping from one thing to the next that we do not allow ourselves to acknowledge how we are feeling, but mindfulness practices offer us these opportunities.

When we are busy all the time we often live in our heads – we have so many thoughts to focus on that we neglect to notice signs that our body is giving us. When we practise mindfulness, it develops the connection between our mind and body, making it easier to recognize signals from the body. Our body can send us warning signals that we are getting overtired, stressed or ill, but if we are living in our heads then we may ignore these signals. Our bodies are trying to protect us, to let us know we need to slow down and look after ourselves. Mindfulness brings us to the here and now – to be in the present and aware of what is happening in and around us.

Practising mindfulness helps to reduce stress and anxiety by inhibiting the overproduction of cortisol in your body. High levels of cortisol make you feel stressed, so lowering them helps you feel calmer. When this happens, you are likely to live your life with greater happiness and balance, because your mind and body are more balanced. When you practise mindfulness, you start to notice and appreciate the small things in life. It is easier to find joy and contentment in small things such as spotting a bird, a beautiful flower or tasting a delicious cup of tea. By finding happiness and being grateful for the small things in life you become happier in general as there are so many small, wonderful things to discover.

By practising mindfulness regularly, you are making a commitment to yourself. Committing to prioritize yourself, even for just a few minutes daily, is important because we deserve to make time for our own self-care and love. When you allow yourself this time it becomes easier to spot when you are thinking negative thoughts about yourself or your situation. Once you have noticed these thought patterns you can choose whether you want to continue thinking in that way or whether you would like to stop. That makes it sound extremely easy, as if you just need to flick a switch and decide that you are not thinking that way now. By simply recognizing when you are thinking in a negative way and saying to yourself, *I choose to think differently*, you will start to make new connections in your brain, which makes it easier for this to happen.

When you start to notice your thoughts and patterns you recognize when you are thinking in a more positive way. You may notice that you can shift your perspective from a negative to a positive thought pattern by standing up and moving. This action sends a message to your brain that you want to change your current situation. If you are having negative thoughts try going to make a cup of tea or coffee or walking around the room. By actively choosing to change your environment you give yourself some space to observe how you are feeling. When you recognize negative thoughts and patterns you have the choice to manage difficulties in a new way. You create new pathways in your brain that offer you the opportunity to respond to what is happening rather than react.

Overall, mindfulness offers you a whole range of benefits, because it:

- supports the training of your attention

- provides opportunities to give yourself time

- is a commitment to yourself

- develops a mind and body connection

- helps you live life with greater happiness and balance

- brings you to the here and now

- reduces stress and anxiety

- changes the structure of the brain

- helps you to manage difficulties in a new way

- gives you time to notice negative thoughts and patterns

The benefits of mindfulness have been thoroughly researched over the last 50 years, especially by Jon Kabat-Zinn, who devised the Mindfulness-Based Stress Reduction course (MBSR).[1] These are some of his findings – people who practised mindfulness regularly:

- were happier

- had more energy

- were less stressed

- felt their lives were more meaningful

- had more control over their lives

- were more likely to see challenges as opportunities rather than as threats

# How I Came to Practise Mindfulness

Over eight years ago, I attended some wellbeing training for staff in our consortium of schools. The hall was filled with teachers, support staff and Headteachers from the local area. It was a cold February morning, and I was not sure what we would be doing. In the busyness of the chattering room, a woman stood up and talked to us about mindfulness and how we could complete an eight-week course based on a book by Mark Williams and Danny Penman called *Mindfulness: A Practical Guide to Finding Peace in a Frantic World*, a book that I subsequently read and reread many times.[2] The facilitator then led us through a couple of short, guided practices. In those few minutes of practice, I focused on my body and my breath. It was as if everything else, all the busyness and hundreds of people were not there. I felt a calmness and stillness. I remember when the practice was over, I mentioned to a colleague that it felt like something special and I wanted to know more about it.

While reading Mark Williams and Danny Penman's book, I followed the suggested practices and listened to the accompanying CD of meditations. At the time, my son was only seven years old and my daughter was nine. I had not taken any time to do anything like this for myself since they were born. My son chose to join me for many of the meditations and we would lie together on the bed listening to the CD. Sometimes my daughter would join us, making the moment even more special. I looked forward to this short amount of time in my day when I would listen to a mindfulness practice either on my own or accompanied by my children.

About a month after starting to practise mindfulness regularly I had a school lesson observation. In the past I was always stressed at the prospect of lesson observations – it felt like I was being judged and I did not want my Headteacher to think that I was not good at my job. This resulted in many days of overplanning one lesson for observation – it would be an all-singing, all-dancing lesson where all aspects of learning were embraced. I always received positive feedback after observations but also knew that they were not a true reflection of an everyday lesson.

This lesson observation was different – I planned a solid lesson and delivered it well. My Headteacher noticed a difference. When she was giving me feedback, she asked what was different – the difference was mindfulness. I did not feel manic about my observed lesson. I was happy to be my authentic self. My everyday teaching is consistent, varied and well-pitched; that is what helps children to make great progress, not all-singing and all-dancing lessons. That lesson observation showed me the true power of mindfulness. Committing to a short practice, which I looked forward to each day, helped create a shift in my perspective, my thoughts and my presentation.

I continued practising mindfulness and found that it was something that I really enjoyed. Then my school decided to run a face-to-face Mindfulness-Based Stress Reduction course. The course was brilliant and eight members of staff participated in it. I enjoyed the sessions and various levels of contemplation, questioning and opportunities to share – the experience was different to when I studied by myself.

I took the course again before attending a teacher training course to become a certified MBSR teacher.[3] I read the research about mindfulness, and I developed a greater understanding of why mindfulness works and the neuroscience behind it.

Since doing the mindfulness teacher training, I have collaboratively taught many groups of staff and parents. Each time we deliver the course the content is the same; however, what individual people take away from it can be quite different – they take from the course what they need at that time. I have also trained to teach children about mindfulness and I regularly build it into my daily teaching to help children develop self-regulation techniques.

Hopefully, by doing some of the mindfulness-based activities in this book, you will find benefits for yourself too. The mindful practices will help you to acknowledge how you are feeling at the time. With practise, you will learn to choose to respond rather than react to situations.

## Understanding Mindfulness

I would like you to imagine a snow globe. Imagine shaking it up so that all the glittery snowflakes are swirling and twirling around. Our minds can be like a snow globe, with our thoughts dashing around like the whirling snowflakes. Our minds may be stormy and wild, but by practising mindfulness, we can stop and notice every snowflake, every thought, and notice as the thoughts start to settle.

Our brains are complex and the autonomic nervous system is made up of two parts: the sympathetic nervous system, which is responsible for our fight-or-flight response, and the parasympathetic nervous system, which is responsible for our rest and digest response. Our brains have developed over generations, but the functions of the autonomic nervous system have remained the same. A long time ago, when our ancestors often had to deal with dangerous threats, such as sabre-toothed tigers, their bodies had to have a quick response to survive. In an instant, they had to make a choice about whether they were going to fight, to stay and confront the tiger, or whether they were going to take flight and flee. Although nowadays we do not have to worry about sabre-toothed tigers, our bodies and minds can be triggered in the same way by lots of different stresses. It could be an upcoming meeting with a parent that causes you stress or dealing with challenging behaviour in the classroom.

Our body can be triggered in the same way it would have been all those years ago. When that happens, our body protects us by doing several things in a chain reaction. When we are triggered, our sympathetic nervous system stimulates our adrenal glands, triggering the release of adrenaline. There are different physical signs in your body that you may notice when this happens. Your pupils dilate to let in more light so that you have better vision, and you can see more of your surroundings. Your skin may become pale or flushed and that's because the blood closest to the surface of the body is reduced as blood is sent to the muscles and the heart so that you are able to respond quickly and run or fight. Your skin can alternate between pale and flushed as blood is sent to the brain. Your body develops its blood-clotting facilities to prevent blood loss in the event of injury. Your heart is likely to beat more rapidly, and your breathing is likely to be affected. Your body is providing you with the oxygen and energy you need to respond rapidly to danger. Another reaction may be trembling, because muscles tense as they are primed for action and this can cause them to tremble or shake.

All these responses helped our ancient ancestors to survive when under threat. Our modern-day stresses can cause the same responses in our bodies now. When I first became an Assistant Headteacher I started leading whole-school assemblies regularly. A 15-minute slot in the school day where I shared a story with a moral, a prayer and a song. In principle it should be something that I did not need to overthink, however, I was really worried about doing the assemblies. Leading up to them and while I was doing them, I had this nervous feeling in my stomach and my breathing was heavier as I tried to remain calm. Other staff in the hall had no idea how anxious I was feeling about leading the assembly. I continue to regularly lead assemblies now, 10 years later, and although they are not something I look forward to doing I am not anxious about them anymore.

Sometimes, depending on the circumstance, the more we are exposed to and have a safe experience of something that makes us feel worried, the power it has over us decreases. The more we do something challenging without being anxious the better we feel. This scenario assumes that you have a safe space to have the experience, but if you feel unsafe in any way then it will not make any difference how much exposure you have to something, you are likely to still be triggered. Our fight-or-flight response is there to protect us when we do not feel safe.

## FIGHT OR FLIGHT

Think about times when you have experienced the fight-or-flight response:

- How did your body react?

- Was it a real or a perceived danger?

- What do you notice when you think about these things?

After your body has been in the fight-or-flight response it is going to be tired. Your body has worked hard to protect you from a danger, whether it is real or perceived, and has directed resources where you needed them. After the threat has passed, your high adrenaline levels plummet, and your body needs to recover. When you have had a stressful day at work for whatever reason, and your body has been triggered into a fight-or-flight response, you are likely to feel exhausted later. Your body would have been sending you signals that you are tired, but if you have ignored them and continued teaching then when you do stop the crash will be greater.

# Autopilot

Have you ever driven home and not really remembered the journey or walked into a room and forgotten why you had gone there? These are examples of when we do things in autopilot mode, things we have done so often that we are unable to recall details. You are not fully present at these times – your mind drifts so you are not present with what you are doing. When you practise mindfulness, you become more aware of your thoughts and actions, and you live more in the present moment, experiencing life as it is happening rather than living in the thoughts in your head.

When we are in autopilot we are acting, doing, interacting but we are not present. Our minds take over and we do things without consciously remembering if we have done them. There are so many times in our day when we do repetitive activities, from cleaning our teeth, doing the washing up, putting on our shoes, to driving to the shops and making the dinner. We have similar tasks that we do repeatedly. These tasks can be completed in autopilot mode. Oftentimes, when we are functioning on autopilot our mind is thinking about other things, things we need to do, plans and worries, and these thoughts take over what we are doing so we are not present in the here and now. We end up missing parts of our lives as a result.

Research from Harvard University found that we are not living in the present for up to 47 per cent of the time – meaning that we are not fully aware for nearly half our lives.[4] Mindfulness trains our minds to focus on the present, on where we are right now. It helps us to be aware of what is happening around us and within us, to notice the decisions and choices that we make every day. Often, we do things because we have always done them or because we think they are expected of us. When you practise mindfulness, you become more aware of your choices, habits and responses. This awareness offers you the opportunity to decide if you want to do things as you always have or if you want to make a conscious decision to do things differently. You have the choice to step out of autopilot and live your life.

Stress is our body's reaction to an event that may be perceived or real. What causes stress in one person might not cause stress in someone else. Our experiences and reactions in the past influence our responses in the present moment. Often, we go into autopilot when we are stressed, and we do things without even thinking about them.

## OVERRIDING AUTOPILOT

There are small steps that you can try if you notice that you are living part of your life on autopilot. You may start really small, like noticing when you are brushing your teeth. When you brush your teeth try to be present for that task and nothing else. You may notice that two minutes of brushing seems to take a longer time than usual. You may notice the sensations of your toothbrush or the taste of your toothpaste. You could try being more present when you brush your hair, get dressed, wash the dishes or drive to work. I know when I first started to do this, I was astonished by how much more I saw and experienced by deciding to be consciously present.

. . . . . . . . . . . . . . . . . . . . . . . . .

The impact of choosing to be present and override autopilot means that you are starting to train your brain to make new neural pathways and make new decisions. You are helping to train your attention, which can have huge benefits. If we train our brains to be more present, we help them become stronger. What we focus our attention on forms stronger connections in our brains. Our brains change and adapt.

## When We Punish Ourselves

There will always be times when something goes wrong in our lives. It could be trivial things like stubbing your toe or taking the wrong exit off a motorway. When things do not go as you hoped then you have the initial pain, for example the pain in your toe after the injury, but you also have the secondary pain that you inflict on yourself by beating yourself up for what happened. With your stubbed toe, you may become cross that someone left something on the floor, or you might get upset and annoyed with yourself for stubbing your toe because you know you were tired and clumsier. Sometimes we take this frustration out on others and sometimes we become frustrated with ourselves. Either way, we are punishing ourselves for a mistake.

If we think about taking the wrong exit off the motorway, we know this is a genuine mistake as we would not deliberately go the wrong way. We already have the nuisance of finding a different route or trying to get back to our original route, but often we also add a layer of shame or guilt onto ourselves, thinking how silly we have been to make this mistake in the first place.

We may also do this with bigger things in our lives and this may have an impact on those around us. It may be that we had a disagreement with a colleague, or we are frustrated with our own child or we have been angered by a situation or conversation. When these interactions happen, they stay with us; it is hard for us to move on from them and we can sometimes then take our frustrations out on others who have not done anything wrong. We may snap at other people or not be our usual selves. This can then create a cycle of guilt about our actions.

When things go wrong in our lives that cause us frustration or upset then it is helpful for us to acknowledge and recognize them. By doing this we are naming what we are feeling, and we are less likely to continue punishing ourselves for an honest mistake. Mistakes make us human – no one is perfect, we all make mistakes. By being aware of our reactions and responses to these situations we can learn more about ourselves and our actions. It may be that you react in a certain way because that was modelled to you as a child, it may be that you are always critical of yourself and expecting perfection. Whatever you notice about yourself is useful, as it helps you decide if you want to continue to respond in the same way in the future. By acknowledging your reactions, you create a pause while you decide how you want to proceed. We cannot stop mistakes from happening, but we can change the inner dialogue we have afterwards. We can choose to be kind to ourselves and those around us. This will then create positive pathways in our brain that make it easier in the future when things do not go as we hoped.

# Being Curious

My first mindfulness teacher often talked about being curious about what you see, hear and feel. When you practise mindfulness – whether it is a formal practice where you commit to a mindfulness exercise for a certain amount of time, or an informal practice where you notice what is happening around or within you – you learn to be more curious about yourself and the world.

Often in mindfulness you may hear the term 'beginner's mind'; this means that you approach something as though it is new to you.[5] You look at something with an openness as if you do not have any previous experience of it. So often we have formed opinions and scenarios in our minds about how things will go. You may find that you catastrophize what may happen, you may tell yourself that you are preparing for the worst-case scenario so that you are ready for anything. When you do this, you are bringing negativity or worry to the situation. When we train to be teachers, we are taught to consider what may go wrong; we are then observed and receive constructive feedback about our lessons, which builds on our need to consider all options. Unfortunately, when this becomes the pattern throughout our lives we lose our curiosity, our excitement and joy in experiencing what is happening in the moment as we are planning for the worst in the future.

# ADOPTING A BEGINNER'S MIND

When things feel unsure or unsafe then it can be harder for us to be curious and adopt a beginner's mind. Maybe start to address this by bringing a curiosity to the smallest things in your life: Be curious when you go for a walk. What can you see? What can you hear? What can you smell? What can you feel? Bringing awareness to each of your senses in turn while doing something as simple as going for a walk will awaken your curiosity. How many times do you go for a walk, but do not consider your surroundings and your experiences as you are occupied with thoughts and worries? By consciously noticing your senses you will develop a beginner's mind.

You may wish to experience being curious about other things in your life, such as eating a meal or snack, doing exercise or having a shower. By focusing your curiosity on everyday tasks, you can experience a beginner's mind and how it makes you feel. I find that when I consciously do this, I am surprised at how calm and present I feel. I find it is then easier to apply this principle to other areas of my life, such as when I am teaching.

We can bring curiosity to all situations. If you are having a discussion or disagreement and, instead of staying firm in your opinion, you become curious about the other person's viewpoint, it can completely change your interaction. This does not mean that you need to change your opinions, but being curious and hearing the other person's perspective and really listening to what they have to say may lead to a more positive interaction. We all feel better if we feel heard and listened to. It also gives us an opportunity to understand another person better. We are more likely to be listened to ourselves or feel we can ask to be listened to if we have modelled that behaviour to others.

## THINGS TO PONDER

- What situations can you bring curiosity to?

- What do you notice when you pay attention in the moment?

- When would having a beginner's mind be useful to you?

# Mindfulness for Pupils

A few years after my general mindfulness training, I trained to be a children's mindfulness teacher. The course I attended had a good balance of theory and practical exercises and it explained the neuroscience clearly. I relished bringing the practices of mindfulness into the classroom. I regularly use mindfulness in school with an individual, a group or with the whole class. Mindfulness gives children self-regulation and self-soothing techniques. It gives them tools that they can use whenever they need them. In my experience, children find mindfulness empowering – a superpower to use whenever they wish.

It is immensely powerful to watch two children who are only six years old helping each other to calm down by using mindfulness or breathing strategies. One day a girl came into class particularly upset – she was having trouble leaving her parents that morning – and another child went up to her and said, 'I can help you do your breathing. I will help you. Do the breathing with me. Let us breathe in together and breathe out together.' The children sat down together and did breathing exercises. The child who was upset calmed quickly and was soon smiling and you could see the sense of pride in the child who had helped. That was such a special moment, watching the children being empowered to help each other. It helps children to know that they have tools to help themselves and others.

Another time, a boy in my class shared how his family's car had broken down while they were on a day trip. He described how his dad was upset and worried about the car. He then told the class how he had shown his dad and the rest of his family how to do some mindfulness techniques and that helped his dad feel better. In a situation that could have felt frightening for that child, he used mindfulness to help himself and his family.

I have seen countless times when children in my classes have used mindfulness strategies to help them self-regulate or guide their friends or peers in regulating themselves. For children to be able to do this they need to be taught simple mindfulness strategies, such as basic breathing techniques, or easy practices, such as listening to what they hear around them. They need to be taught how these practices help them; for example, if they breathe in for the count of three and out for the count of five then they will feel calmer, and this breathing helps when they are feeling cross or upset. Children need time to practise these techniques and many short revision sessions to help them remember.

When my class were going to join in our whole-school sports day, with parents watching, we went through this three : five breathing technique. We practised doing it as a whole class, and then they taught and explained it to visiting adults. They also practised talking it through with a friend. Each time we did a short session on breathing we reinforced that it was good when you felt worried or upset. We also talked about it being a superpower because no one knows you are doing it, but it can make you feel much better quickly. When it came to sports day, some children said they were feeling nervous and others reminded their friends to do their breathing. By teaching pupils techniques like this we are empowering them to regulate themselves and recognize that it is normal to feel big emotions. For this to be taught effectively, the teachers themselves need to feel comfortable with the techniques.

Once children have learned a few mindfulness strategies they can use them to support their learning. When they feel overwhelmed, for example in a test situation, they have a technique they can use. If they are upset for whatever reason, by using a mindfulness strategy they have a way to become aware of their feelings. It is worth teaching a few different techniques as children can then choose which ones they prefer.

# CHAPTER 5

# Short Mindfulness
# Practices

*'By changing the way in which you see the world,*
*you effectively change the world around you.'*

ANDY PUDDICOMBE

In this chapter you will find short mindfulness practices that you can try out and come back to as many times as you wish or need. You are likely to find that you prefer certain practices and that you come back to the same practice many times. You may find that how you are feeling or what you are experiencing at a certain time determines which practice you prefer. I invite you to try them all to find the practices that suit you best.

Start with this short grounding practice.

## SHORT GROUNDING PRACTICE

This practice is very quick but helps you to connect back to your body and can take you away from thoughts in your head. It is a practice that you could do anywhere, and no one would realize that you are doing it. When you do this practice, you bring awareness to your body and help to create a short pause which then allows you to proceed with what you want to do with more clarity.

- I invite you to start the practice by being aware of where you are sitting before bringing attention to your breathing. You can use your breathing to anchor yourself and to feel more present in the moment. Your breath is always present and it can support you when you want to feel more grounded.

- Now, take a moment to settle more comfortably on your chair.

- Sit upright, slightly away from the back of the chair, allowing your spine to support itself. Keep your legs uncrossed, gently placing both feet on the floor if you're able to do so.

- Perhaps close your eyes or lower your gaze, whatever works for you.

- Notice where your body comes into contact with the surface of the chair and floor. Sense where your legs touch the chair, and the soles of your feet connect to the floor. Rest your hands in your lap if that feels comfortable.

- Bring your awareness back to your breathing, just breathing normally and naturally. Breathing in and breathing out.

- Notice the movements of your body and the physical sensations. Become aware of where you feel the breath most in your body; maybe it is in your nostrils. Maybe you can feel the cold sensation as you breathe in through your nose and the warmer sensation as you breathe out. Maybe you can feel the rise and the fall of your chest or abdomen.

- There is no need to control your breathing in any way. Just allow yourself to experience what is happening in this moment, as your body follows its natural rhythm of breathing in and breathing out.

- You're not trying to alter or change anything, just notice what is happening. Notice what you're experiencing in this moment.

- Your mind might start to wander, which it is likely to do; maybe you will start daydreaming, planning or worrying. When this happens, just notice what's happened and gently bring your attention back, with kindness, to the part of the body you're focusing on, where you feel your breath most strongly.

- Perhaps you've noticed how, after your outbreath, your body will naturally take the next breath in all by itself. There's nothing for you to do in that moment. Just simply notice your breath flow in and out like the waves of the sea.

- As you come to the end of the practice, lower your chin. Open your eyes if they've been closed, and let your eyes slowly get used to what's around you. Take a few moments to stretch if that makes you feel better.

. . . . . . . . . . . . . . . . . . . . . . . . .

The more that you do this simple grounding practice the easier you will find it to use your breath as an anchor. It becomes easier to notice your breathing and focus on it when you feel you want to either slow down, calm down or take time to pause. The practice allows you to take a moment before continuing with what you were doing. It allows your nervous system to quieten, which makes it easier for you to deal with the situation that you are in. This can be a great practice to do when you first return from work, helping you to transition from work to home.

# Making Time for Mindfulness

Taking time to be mindful, even if it is just for a minute, is worthwhile. Sometimes you need to make time in your day to be mindful because things become overwhelming or there's too much going on.

It can be hard to find the time to do a long practice for maybe half an hour. Luckily, there are lots of benefits from just taking a mindful minute. Just taking one minute can make a real difference. It can help you to connect with how you feel in your body and to recognize what's going on around you. This connection may help you decide what you want to do next. You can take a mindful minute in your day whenever you need it. And most of the time, you can do it without anyone else realizing what you're doing. So even if you're in a busy meeting, or you're in the middle of the classroom and you just need to take a moment, try doing a mindful minute. Sometimes it's better for you and everybody around you if you take that time.

## ONE MINDFUL MINUTE

The scripts below show you how to take one mindful minute. Just follow a script and see what a difference it makes to your day.

### Feet on the Floor

- Start by placing both feet firmly on the ground.

- Feel your feet on the ground.

- Feel and connect to the ground.

- Take all your attention to your feet and slowly breathe in and out.

- Breathe in and breathe out.

- Just breathe and concentrate on your feet for 20 to 30 seconds.

- At the end of that time take a moment to recognize how you are feeling. Hopefully, you will feel different now than you did at the start of the minute.

## Listening to Sounds

In this mindful-minute script, we are just going to listen to everything that we hear around us.

- Start by taking a moment to stop whatever you are doing. You can choose to sit or stand to do this practice.

- What sounds can you hear?

- What sounds can you hear that are close to you?

- Where is one of these close sounds coming from?

- Is it a sound you like?

- What is the furthest sound that you can hear?

- Just focus on the sounds that you can hear, not worrying about anything else other than listening to the sounds.

- When you pause to listen to sounds what do you notice?

Even if you are in the middle of a classroom, and if everybody is safe at that moment, you can do this exercise because you can listen to what's going on around you. There is nothing to stop you just pausing and listening. Your attention is still present. Alternatively, you can invite the children to listen with you, helping them to be mindful too. You're still able to do your job, but you are also able to look after yourself by just pausing for a moment and listening.

## Awareness of Touch

Another short practice you can do when you only have time for a mindful minute is to be aware of touch. When we focus on what we feel through the sense of touch we focus our attention, and this may help us to feel calmer and more in control.

- What parts of your body are making contact with the floor or a chair?

- Can you notice the touch of your clothes on your skin?

- Can you focus on your thumb rubbing against your finger?

Focusing on these areas of touch can help to bring our attention to the present moment and can feel quite soothing and reassuring.

# Mindful Movement

Any daily movement brings the opportunity to bring mindful awareness to that movement. You may be thinking, *why do I want to bring mindful awareness to movement?* The simple answer is that it helps us to be present and aware of what our body is doing and experiencing. It helps us to be present in that moment in time. It is easy for our minds to wander and for thoughts to constantly bombard our brains, which can be exhausting. By focusing our attention, we allow ourselves to fully enjoy what we are doing and give our minds a rest from overthinking. When we are prone to overthinking and our minds are constantly trying to solve one problem after the next, we can feel tired. By drawing our awareness to the present mindfully, we allow our minds to rest, and problems become easier to solve. Have you ever been so consumed with a physical activity that it's not possible to think about anything other than what you are doing at that time? This is what I experience with karate: I have to be completely focused on my movements and actions. At the end of a session, I am calmer, as my mind has been focused on one thing.

## MOVE MINDFULLY

You can practise mindful movement by simply walking on the spot. Noticing which part of each foot comes into contact with the floor first, noticing if there is movement in your arms. You could then try walking faster on the spot or marching; does the same part of your foot touch the ground first? Do you feel the movement in a different part of your legs? Maybe try jogging on the spot and compare how that feels. You don't need to do these exercises for a long time but try to be fully aware of what you are doing and where you notice movement in your body.

Mindful movement could involve bringing awareness to movements that you do every day. It could be that you decide to notice each time you sit in a chair. Do you feel the front of your thighs tighten, your stomach pull in as you lower yourself down? How does your body feel while sitting in the chair? What do you feel when you stand up? It could be noticing the movements of your hands when you do the washing up, the sensation of the water on your skin, the movements your hands make holding and washing, the rotation of your wrists.

You could choose to be mindful while doing exercise. If you enjoy yoga or Pilates, notice the speed and control of your movements. If you like swimming, try bringing awareness to the movements of your arms, hands, legs and feet, being aware of when you breathe and how that feels. If you enjoy hiking, running or cycling, consider the movements that your body makes and what you feel. How do you feel before making a movement, during that movement and when you have finished?

. . . . . . . . . . . . . . . . . . . . . . .

## THINGS TO PONDER

- When can you bring awareness to your movements during the day?

- What do you notice when you think about making a movement?

- How do you feel before, during and after a movement?

# Considering Other Perspectives

There may be times when you need to have an awkward conversation with a colleague. You may need to speak to them about something you feel unable to do at that time, or you may need to talk to them about something that you feel apprehensive about. Any interaction of this sort is likely to make you feel a bit nervous. You don't know how the other person is going to react; it can feel unpredictable. It may be that you know a colleague has been upset by a situation and you are going to talk to them and see how they are. You may have the best intentions to check in on someone, but the conversation might feel awkward.

## OTHER PEOPLES' PERSPECTIVES

It may be a useful exercise to consider another person's perspective because this helps us realize that we never really know what another person is dealing with at any one time.

Think about the person you have been interacting with or need to interact with: Consider how they look, who they might have spoken to that day, how they might be feeling and what happened to them that day. Think about what their life might be like, what their childhood might have been like.

Consider aspects of this person to help you understand that how someone reacts to you in a moment is not necessarily about you. There are many things that make a person who they are: the experiences, lessons and love they have received in their life.

Sometimes when we ask our work colleagues how they are, after we know they have dealt with something challenging, they may feel that we are questioning their ability to cope. At these times, even though our intention is to support them, we may feel that our colleague has perceived our offer as another challenge. It is useful for us to bear in mind that we never really know what is going on in someone else's life.

When you are communicating with an upset parent of a child with Special Educational Needs and Disabilities (SEND), understanding their perspective is useful. SEND parents have probably had to fight to get their child diagnosed, then had to fight for support for their child and for people to understand their child's specific needs. If the child has complex needs, as teachers we may sometimes underestimate what is upsetting the parent. When you consider the level of challenge that the parent faces every day it becomes easier to see things from their viewpoint. As teachers, we work hard to understand all the children that we teach. It may feel like the parents do not understand how much work we do to adapt our lesson plans to take their child's individual needs into consideration. But it may be that our viewpoint needs to shift – this is part of our job.

Parents of SEND children with complex needs have to think about these needs all the time and they then put their trust in us; it's understandable that sometimes they need us to prove they can trust us. Children with complex SEND, and children who have limited speech or communication, are particularly vulnerable. Understandably, their parents worry about whether we will give their child the same nurturing that they would. It can be hard sometimes to know exactly what the child may need or want, but our judgement will improve as we get to know the child.

As teachers, we gradually come to know the children in our class very well. We spot when they are acting out of character or seem a bit pale, but we will never know a child as well as their parents. Parents are the experts of their children, and they trust us to look after their children. It is fine for them to question us to get clarity, even though that may feel like we are being judged. In these situations, seek out colleagues whom you can speak to and share how you are feeling and what has happened.

Think about what the parent may have been going through before they interacted with you.

# STOP

When things are getting too much or I have been pushed so that I feel I may react in a way I wouldn't choose, one simple mindful practice that I use often is STOP, which stands for:

- **S**top

- **T**ake a breath

- **O**bserve

- **P**roceed

When you feel that things are getting too much for whatever reason, you can choose to stop what you are doing for a moment and consciously focus on your breathing. Then observe your emotions, thoughts and any sensations that you have in your body before you proceed with what you were doing.

This simple practice is useful in many scenarios and I regularly use it whilst teaching. It is a good practice when a pupil is demonstrating challenging behaviour and you know that they will respond better if you are calmer. Giving yourself just a few moments to check in with how you are feeling, before dealing with how someone else is feeling, helps you to know you approached a situation in the best way possible and it ensures you protect yourself.

STOP is a useful practice when you are feeling snappy, and you know your patience is shorter for whatever reason. By having a brief pause to stop, you give yourself a bit of space and it becomes easier to process and make decisions. I have two teenagers and I have found this is a beneficial practice to do myself when they have heightened emotions for any reason, as it helps me to stay more grounded and therefore I can support them better.

# Meditation

Meditation is a useful mindfulness tool. In this short meditation practice, you bring awareness to what you are experiencing at the time. You then narrow your focus to your breathing before expanding your awareness to your whole body. It is sometimes useful to visualize this practice as an hourglass, with a wide focus, narrowing in the middle and then expanding out at the end.

## THREE-STEP MINI MEDITATION

### Step One: Awareness

Bring yourself into the present moment by deliberately adopting a tall and dignified posture. If possible, close your eyes or lower your gaze.

Then ask yourself the following questions:

– What is my experience right now?

– What am I thinking?

- What am I feeling?

- What am I aware of in my body?

Acknowledge and register your experience – whatever is here for you in this moment, even if it is something you would prefer was not there.

## Step Two: Narrowing

Then focus your full attention on your breathing, on each breath in and each breath out, as they follow one after the other. Your breath can function as an anchor to bring you into the present moment and help you tune into a state of awareness and stillness. Focus on the centre of the body when you are breathing.

## Step Three: Expanding

Expand the field of your awareness around your breathing, so that it includes a sense of your body, your posture, your facial expression and anything you are aware of. Bring acceptance to all that's arising in your body with kindness.

. . . . . . . . . . . . . . . . . . . . . . . .

This short practice helps us to connect with our current experiences and move out of autopilot mode by helping to bring awareness to a moment in our lives. The key skill in using mindfulness is to maintain awareness in the moment. Nothing else. We are not trying to pressurize ourselves to relax, we are not trying to change what we are experiencing in any moment – we are learning to accept what is already here with kindness and awareness.

# Scanning the Body

The first main practice that Jon Kabat-Zinn includes in his eight-week mindfulness course, which is now taught around the world, is the body scan.[1] You can do the body scan while lying down or sitting in a chair. Throughout the body scan, you are taking your attention to different parts of your body and noticing if you feel any sensations there. Some people find it easy to take their attention to different parts of their body and sense if they feel a tingling, numbness, aching or nothing at all. Other people struggle to focus on just one part of the body at a time. Often, we spend so much time thinking in our heads that we don't pay attention to the rest of our bodies. Our bodies are always sending us signals and messages to let us know if something feels uncomfortable or not right. When we spend so much time thinking in our heads, we can miss the signals our bodies are giving us until they are screaming at us that something isn't right.

The body scan is a great practice to do if you notice something doesn't feel right in your body – taking time to slow down and really notice what is going on in your body can be very beneficial. It is also very useful if you know you are overthinking and want a chance to focus your attention somewhere else.

When you do the body scan don't worry if you find it difficult to keep your attention on the part of the body you are trying to focus on. Our minds are so used to wandering and thinking that they will try to take over – you may notice you are thinking many thoughts whilst you are trying to do the body scan. This is very normal! Don't give yourself a hard time when this happens. See if you notice when your mind wanders, recognize that your mind has wandered and then gently take your focus back to the part of the body you had reached in the scan. There is no need to start again from the beginning, just go back to focusing on the last part of the body scan you remember. You are likely to find that you need to do this many times and that's usual. You are learning to train your brain to pay attention. The more often you do this scan the stronger your neural pathways become. Jon Kabat-Zinn compares bringing our attention back to our mindfulness practice to training a puppy: We need to be gentle and loving to ourselves, just as we would with a puppy, bringing our attention back with kindness.

# BODY SCAN

When you first try a body scan meditation, experiment with doing it lying down or sitting in a chair. Don't be surprised if you fall asleep while lying down. It's not the intention of the body scan to fall asleep but you may find this happens as your body and mind relax.

- Start the body scan by getting yourself into a position that you will be comfortable in for the length of the practice. Gently close your eyes and notice your breathing. Begin by taking all your attention down to your feet.

- Bring all your attention to your feet.

- Start with the big toe on your left foot, then concentrate on each toe in turn.

- Move your attention to the sole of your foot, the heel, the arch and the ball.

- Then, think about the top of your foot and then your ankle.

- Do you feel any sensations in your ankle?

- Move your attention up to your lower leg, the back of your calf, your shin.

- Take a deeper breath before moving your attention to your left knee.

- Then to the top of your left leg.

- Then do the same with your right side, starting with the big toe on your right foot. Follow the same sequence of taking your attention to focus on one part of your body at a time. Notice if you feel any sensations in each part of your body, just noticing what is there for you, then moving on to the next part.

- When you have moved your attention up both legs, bring your attention to your hips, lower back, middle of your back and top of your back.

- Next, bring your attention to your shoulders before focusing on the top of your left arm, your elbow and then your lower left arm.

- Focus next on your left wrist, the back of your left hand, the thumb followed by each finger and the palm of the hand.

- Take similar attention down your right arm and hand.

- Next focus on the back of your neck, back of your head, top of your head and each of the features on your face.

- You may like to finish by bringing awareness to the whole of your body at the same time, before bringing your attention back to your breathing.

When you finish your body scan take a moment to stretch out and notice how you are feeling. It is your decision how long it takes you to scan through your body and if you decide to do a complete body scan or just focus on a targeted area.

. . . . . . . . . . . . . . . . . . . . . . . . .

# Breath Work

One of the quickest and most accessible mindfulness practices is noticing the breath. We breathe every second of every day but most of the time we don't think about our breathing; it is something we do without conscious awareness. As we breathe continually, it is great to focus on our breath and bring awareness to it when we want to slow our thoughts or emotions.

## NOTICE YOUR BREATH

Take a moment to notice your breathing. Where do you feel the breath when you take a deep breath in? Do you feel it in your chest or your belly? When we are babies, we naturally breathe into our bellies but sometimes as we get older, we breathe more into our chests.

To breathe more into your belly try placing a hand on your belly and see if you can feel your belly expanding and contracting as you breathe. Imagine your belly filling with air like a balloon as you breathe in and then deflating as you breathe out. Try doing this to help slow your breathing down if you are feeling agitated, angry or upset.

I teach my pupils three : five breathing, so they breathe in for the count of three and out for the count of five. When we have a longer exhale than inhale it helps us to calm down. It is a useful self-regulation strategy for the children to know, but it works just as well for adults too. If, for whatever reason, my class is feeling bubbly, and I would like the energy in the room to calm down then I will lead a breathing technique with the class. I join in the breathing technique when I do it with the class, and I encourage any adults in the room to join in as well. It helps everyone to enjoy a calmer environment.

# BREATHING SCRIPT

The following breathing practice can be as long or short as you have time for or feel comfortable doing it. Decide how long you wish to spend on each section of this mindfulness breathing script.

Start by making yourself comfortable in a seated position with your feet firmly on the floor. Take a few moments to settle into this position, maybe having a wiggle around until you feel comfortable. Allow your eyes to close or gently settle your gaze looking down. Feel your feet on the floor and your legs against the chair. Roll your shoulders back and just notice your natural breath. Notice your breath coming in and out of your body.

Try taking a deeper breath and see what you notice. Where do you feel the breath in your body? Focus on where you notice your breath for a minute or so. Feel how your body moves to accommodate your breath coming in and how it changes as your breath goes out. Do you notice any other parts of your body as you breathe in or out?

If your mind starts to wander while you are doing this practice, that is completely normal; just notice that your mind has wandered and gently bring it back to focusing on the breath. You may notice that your mind keeps wandering and that's okay, you are not doing anything wrong. Just encourage yourself to come back to focusing on the breath.

Try following your breath as it enters your nostrils and moves down the back of your throat and further down into your body. See if you can observe the exhale as it moves from your body and up your throat and out of your nose. You may notice that your nostrils feel the cooler air entering your body as you breathe in and the warmer air leaving as you breathe out. You may wish to spend a few minutes focusing your attention on your nostrils as the air enters and exits.

Notice the sensations in your nose when you breathe. Spend a few minutes just focusing your attention on your breath as it comes into your body. Does it feel smooth or jagged? What do you feel in your nostrils? Once you have done this you can then switch your focus to your breath as it leaves your body. What do you notice about your outbreath? Where does your outbreath start? How does your body feel when your breath goes out? Spend a few minutes focusing on your breath leaving your body.

. . . . . . . . . . . . . . . . . . . . . . . .

All the breath practices in this section can be completed as individual short practices or you might like to combine them to make a longer practice.

## THINGS TO PONDER

- What do you notice when you focus on your breathing?

- Is there a difference in your breathing at the start and end of a practice?

# Practising Loving Kindness

When we practise loving kindness, we are being compassionate to ourselves and others. We have the chance to express kindness to ourselves and send it to others. I find this is a great practice to do when I'm worried about somebody else or when I'm feeling tired or run down.

## LOVING KINDNESS

Start by getting into a comfortable position, rolling your shoulders back and taking a few deep breaths. Close your eyes if you feel that is right for you. Take a moment to scan your body from the tips of your toes to the top of your head to see if you have any discomfort or if you are holding any tension. In this meditation you will be repeating phrases to yourself, starting with: *May I be well*. Repeat that same phrase over in your head, letting it sink in, and recognize how it makes you feel when you repeat the phrase. Here are some alternative phrases that you may like to try or combine the phrases one after the other:

*May I be well.*

*May I be peaceful.*

*May I be happy.*

*May I be filled with joy.*

You can then move on to send loving kindness to someone who is close to you. Imagine clearly in your mind the person to whom you would like to send loving kindness. Think about the way they look, their mannerisms, their unique qualities. Then say these phrases either out loud or in your head as you continue to think about this special person:

*May you be well.*

*May you be peaceful.*

*May you be happy.*

*May your life be filled with joy.*

You may wish to stop the practice there or you can choose to extend it further by sending loving kindness to a wider group of people. You could choose people who are special to you, people who you work with, people in your community or anyone else you choose. It may even be that you choose to send loving kindness to a pet. Imagine these people or pets in your mind. Imagine them forming a circle around you. Think about how they look and their mannerisms. Again, either say these phrases or voice them in your head:

*May you all be well.*

*May you all be peaceful.*

*May you all be happy.*

*May your lives be filled with joy.*

You may choose to extend this meditation further to include people who you don't know so well or people who you find it difficult to be around. Sending loving kindness to this group of people helps to develop your compassion, while also removing some of the negative energy that you may hold towards certain people for whatever reason. Choose the people who you wish to include, and recognize how you feel when you think about them. Say the following phrases whilst thinking about them:

*May you be well.*

*May you be peaceful.*

*May you be happy.*

*May your life be filled with joy.*

Take a few moments after you have finished the meditation, and breathe into your body. Feel the breath coming in and out of your body. Reflect on how you are feeling and if anything came up for you as you thought about sending loving kindness to yourself or to others.

. . . . . . . . . . . . . . . . . . . . . .

Loving kindness can be a great practice to do when you are driving home from work and you are stuck in traffic. It can be easy to feel frustrated during these times, as though your time is being wasted while you wait for the cars to move. Next time you are stuck in traffic consider sending loving kindness to the people you see around you. I imagine zapping people with loving kindness when I do this exercise. For example, looking at a nearby bus and thinking, *all the people on the bus, may you all be well,* or thinking about the person stuck behind you, *may you be happy.* I find whenever I do this, I feel calmer and happier, as I am spreading a bit of love and kindness in the world rather than being frustrated about being stuck in traffic. I find this is also a good practice to think in my head before a meeting with a parent. If I need to have a difficult conversation with a parent, thinking about them and saying in my mind, *may you be well,* helps me to go into the conversation in a calmer manner and I know I have in mind the best intentions for them and their children.

## THINGS TO PONDER

- Who would you send loving kindness to?

- How does it feel to send loving kindness to yourself?

- What do you notice when you carry out a loving kindness practice?

# Take Time to Process

When you want to be more productive or when things are feeling too much then you need to pause – stop for a moment, and give your brain and body time to reconnect with each other. Often when we want to get lots done and our brain is in overdrive, flitting from one idea to the next, we may find that our bodies cannot keep up with what we are doing. We may find that if we are typing something we keep making mistakes or if we are writing we miss out words. It is the same thing that happens to pupils when they are writing – our brains work faster than our bodies and our bodies struggle to keep up. We can feel wired with so many ideas that we jump from one idea to the next without giving ourselves time to settle on one because we fear losing the next idea. When this happens, we are buzzing with ideas but unless we can calm our minds down then it is hard for us to process everything we are thinking at the same time.

A similar thing can happen when we are tired or overwhelmed – we are trying hard to process and remember lots of information, but it can feel too much, and we end up achieving very little. We need to consciously pause and slow down – which can feel like a very difficult thing to do when there is a lot on our plate. By consciously pausing, we allow our brain time to process, and we give ourselves some breathing space to think more clearly.

# PAUSE, PRIORITIZE, PROCEED

I would like you to consciously stop what you are doing, right now, even for just a minute, and allow yourself to take some slow deep breaths, with your body still. Feel your feet on the floor and just be still for a minute.

Once you have paused you can then prioritize – decide what is either the most important or most impactful thing that you need to do. Write a list of all the things that need doing, that are turning round and round in your head, so you do not forget them. By writing it all down you know you have a visual reminder and some of those items will stop looping in your mind, because you no longer need to worry about forgetting them.

When you have your list, I would like you to choose one thing that would relieve some pressure from you if you did it. If you are not sure what to prioritize, choose the things that will have the biggest impact on supporting your wellbeing, because when you feel better you will find it easier to focus on what has the most impact on pupil learning. The tasks that have the least impact on your wellbeing and on pupil learning should go to the bottom of the list. These tasks will keep going to the bottom of the list, and that is okay. Maybe you need to question if the tasks that are not supporting you or your pupils are beneficial.

The next step in Pause, Prioritize, Proceed, is to proceed. Complete the task you have prioritized then proceed with anything else you need or want to do. You can follow this cycle when you want to be more productive but you are struggling to focus on one task, or you are overthinking or procrastinating. It may be that you are feeling overwhelmed and that everything feels too much. By pausing, prioritizing what you want to do and then proceeding, you will let yourself stop and reflect and then focus on one task. It will help to slow your thinking down and make things feel more achievable.

## THINGS TO PONDER

- Do you need to pause?

- Which tasks would you benefit from prioritizing because they will make a difference to you when they are completed?

- Which tasks will have the most impact if you do them?

- How do you feel after trying Pause, Prioritize, Proceed?

- Have you been more productive or more in control after using this method?

# CHAPTER 6

# Mindful Awareness

*'While mindfulness does not necessarily
change what is happening, it changes our
relationship to what is happening.'*

SHAUNA SHAPIRO

This quote by Shauna Shapiro may help us develop a greater understanding about why it is beneficial for us to develop mindful awareness. Although being mindful does not change what is happening to us or around us, it changes our relationship to what is happening by encouraging us to notice our thoughts and feelings. We learn to recognize how situations make us feel and this gives us more choice about how we want to respond. When we consciously acknowledge situations, it changes how we approach things, how we react and the choices we make. Being mindfully aware is like a superpower – it offers you options about how you want to be.

In this chapter we will explore different aspects of mindful awareness; we will notice our thoughts and our feelings so we can start to be aware of patterns. We will look for the good, think about gratitude and experience the benefits of being in nature, as these give us micro boosts of feeling good that can help to shift negative thinking. We will consider what sustains us and what drains us, what builds us up and what pulls us down. If we build opportunities that sustain us and make us happy into our lives then our day-to-day routines may feel more balanced and manageable.

## Noticing Our Thoughts

Have you ever stopped to notice your thoughts? We think about things all the time; even when we are doing one thing we may have thoughts about something else. There are many sayings about how our thoughts become our reality. When we give a thought our time and space we allow it to grow.

Many of the thoughts we have about ourselves are negative. We all have a negative bias in our brains that may sometimes feel hard to override. The first thing we need to do is notice our thoughts. Observe your self-talk. What things do you say to yourself? Are the things you say to yourself positive? Often, we are in a cycle of speaking negatively to ourselves and we do it so often that we think this is normal and that it is fine to be unkind in our self-talk. We do not need to be unkind to ourselves. We would never speak to a friend or a pupil the way we speak to ourselves. Maybe it is time to change that – consider what you are doing to yourself each time you have a negative thought that is putting you down.

Whatever we think about becomes our reality; our thoughts are what consume us and they become our life. It can help to think about our thoughts as if they were floating down a river – we can see them, and it is for us to decide if we want to give them our energy. What we give our attention to, our energy to, will grow stronger. We have a choice about whether to focus on the negative thoughts or whether to focus on the positive thoughts.

You may find all or most of your thoughts are negative and it is hard to stop these thoughts from coming. Our negative thoughts are repetitive and we need to stop that thought train. One way is to recognize and acknowledge the thought; for example, I may become critical about myself for how I handled a conversation with a parent. By recognizing and naming the thought, I have acknowledged it, and then it is easier to move past it because I have taken some of the power away from the thought. Recognizing and noticing when we are having negative thoughts can help us to acknowledge what we are thinking and then we can choose if we want to let that go. Can we send that thought sailing down our metaphorical river? Once we have acknowledged our negative thoughts, we can let them go and be more conscious about what we want to think about.

Recognizing our thoughts and realizing when we are thinking negative thoughts can take some practice. We may be in the habit of being negative and putting ourselves down. We do it all the time, so we do not realize we are doing it. By consciously noticing what we are doing we interrupt this negative cycle, which then allows us to choose something different. If we first notice negative thought patterns and then name them, we acknowledge them. Next, we can take it a step further and actively choose to think about something positive. This can be a small positive thought, such as looking forward to your dinner that night, or noticing how lovely it is when the sun shines through the window. By consciously choosing a positive thought you are reducing the repetitiveness of the negative thoughts.

## THINGS TO PONDER

- Are you speaking to yourself as you would a friend?

- What do you notice when you observe your thoughts?

- What happens when you choose positive thoughts?

# Thoughts Create Our Reality

Mindfulness encourages us to recognize the power of our thoughts. What we think about has a huge impact on how we feel and the life we lead. We have tens of thousands of thoughts every day – which seems mind-blowing in itself. According to the National Science Foundation, 95 per cent of our thoughts are repetitive – meaning that we are having the same thoughts over and over again within a day.[1] These thoughts become the soundtrack to our day and they will help define what kind of day that we have. The National Science Foundation also found that 80 per cent of our daily thoughts are negative thoughts. What overwhelming statistics to consider. If we have that many negative thoughts and repetitive negative thoughts, we are using them to write the story of our lives – the thoughts we create become our reality.

When I wake up having not slept well, or I do not feel refreshed in the morning, I notice those negative, repetitive thought patterns more easily. This is when I decide how I would like to be that day. I may say to myself things like, 'Today I choose to be happy; I choose to remain calm; I choose to enjoy my day'. I might also add things that are playing on my mind and say things like, 'I choose not to worry about...'. The impact that this short, silent exercise has on my outlook amazes me every time. Simply recognizing and choosing the thoughts in my head makes a difference.

You can reduce repetitive negative thought patterns by acknowledging them, but not giving them any more energy. For example, if I notice that I'm worrying about speaking to a parent after school, I say to myself that I know I am worried about speaking to the parent and then observe how that thought then often leaves me. By registering a negative thought in your mind you will not need to keep reminding yourself about it. If you follow that with a positive thought, then the negative thought will become weaker. Your positive thought might be something you are looking forward to, something that you enjoyed recently or something you are grateful for – all these positive thoughts help you to reframe how you are thinking and take power away from negative thoughts. The more you practise doing this, the easier it becomes, and the quicker you notice the negative thoughts, the sooner you reduce them.

If you realize that someone is having repetitive worries that they are talking about, you can help them notice their negative thought patterns. By asking that person directly about their worries and whether it would help to talk about them, you are helping that person to acknowledge their negative thoughts and you can aid them in considering positives about the situation or something else in their life.

# Decide to Be Positive

There is lots of research into positive psychology.[2] What makes someone happy? Part of what makes anyone happy is that they choose to be happy; they make a conscious decision to be positive. I think that teachers do this regularly for others. We may make a conscious decision to help a certain pupil who we know is struggling – we may decide that we are going to be available to help that one individual who is having a hard time. We may think about what that child likes, spend time speaking to that child and help them feel better about themselves. What if we did the same for ourselves? What if we consciously decided to do something that we liked, or talk to someone who we enjoy talking to? What a difference that would make to us.

Every day when we wake up, we make a choice about how we want to be that day. Do we want to embrace life and be happy or moan about all the things we need to do? When we choose to be positive the difference to our experience can be remarkable. Whatever choice we make, whether to be positive or not, has an impact on everyone around us. Our happiness is infectious to those around us. We are likely to help lift the spirits of others just by being positive ourselves. Unfortunately, we may also have a negative impact on those around us with our mood and presence. Bearing this in mind, think about the difference you can have in your teaching day with a positive outlook – how you will promote that for your pupils and what a great environment that would create for you and your class.

I find playing a song I like in the car in the morning is a great way to feel good – singing along in the car often continues as humming down the corridor as I walk through school. Listening to music that we like has been proven to increase our dopamine levels. Dopamine helps us to feel good, experience satisfaction and increases motivation. When you are lacking in motivation or want to feel happier, try blasting out one of your favourite songs to lift you up. At other times I prefer it to be really quiet in the car and think about what I am grateful for on the way to work. Both of these simple exercises can make a huge difference to my day and the day of those around me.

How you present yourself to the people around you can have an impact on you, your relationships and those close to you. If we are happy and upbeat then we help others to feel the same; this means the people that they encounter are also likely to feel happier – it has a ripple effect. In the same way, if we are negative and down then people near us will notice that too, and that will also then affect the people with whom they come into contact.

We have choices and can choose to be cross and angry about something and hold onto it or we can choose to recognize how we are feeling, acknowledge it and then choose to move on from it. It is important to recognize our feelings, but we can also decide how long we want to hold on to those feelings. Will we feel better if we speak to someone, get things off our chest and then move on? Is it something that we can resolve ourselves? Is it something that will still make us cross if we think about it a week from now? Sometimes, by asking ourselves these questions we can start to consider whether it is something we can let go of, or if we are justified in continuing to feel cross about it.

If we think about the ripple effect and how one person's happiness can make everyone around them feel happier, then maybe we need to think about the people with whom we spend our time and energy. Surrounding yourself with people who make you feel good will help you feel better and help you pass that feeling on to others around you.

# Noticing How You Are Feeling

Our moods and feelings fluctuate, and this may be influenced by a number of factors. There will be times in the week or term when, for whatever reason, you do not feel your best. You may know the reason why you are feeling low; for instance, you may have had an injury, an illness or you know it is due to hormonal changes. You may recognize that you are tired and run-down. At other times, you may be feeling great, and everything seems a bit easier. The balance between home and school is easier when everything feels good; teaching feels easier and you feel better about yourself.

Being able to recognize how you are feeling helps you understand more about yourself and what you need at different times. There will be times when you feel great, and you are able to support and encourage others. There will also be times when you do not feel your best and then you may need to focus on yourself first.

When you recognize that you may be feeling down, or that you are tired, it is important to acknowledge this rather than pushing on through. When you acknowledge what you are feeling then you can choose how you want to proceed. If your mood is lower for whatever reason, think about things that make you happy. Maybe spending a few minutes with a pet, sitting and having a hot drink you enjoy or speaking to a friend.

It is important to recognize if you are in a downward cycle of not feeling good. If you find that you are feeling low most of the time, then I encourage you to speak to someone – a colleague at school, a member of the leadership team, a friend or someone else you trust. It may help you to go to the doctor and discuss how you are feeling, or ring an organization such as the Samaritans or the Education Support Partnership Charity, which is there for the wellbeing of school staff, teachers and leaders. You will find their contact details at the back of this book *(see page 222)*. When you are feeling low, depressed or anxious you are not alone and there is support that you can access.

## THINGS TO PONDER

- How are you feeling?

- Would you feel better if you spoke to someone or got support?

# Gratitude

The practice of gratitude is noticing what we are grateful for in our lives or in a moment in time. When we practise gratitude, we shift to a more positive mindset as we consider what makes us thankful. By practising gratitude, you are choosing to actively think about positive aspects of your life and what you are thankful for; this can help to create a shift in your perspective and help you to feel better about your life. It can increase your feelings of abundance as you recognize what you already have and how lucky you are. At its most basic level, you may be grateful for having a bed to sleep in and food to eat – something that not everyone can take for granted. Focusing on what you are thankful for helps to reduce your feelings of fear and anxiety as you choose to focus on good things.

Studies have shown that regularly considering what you are grateful for increases your self-esteem and makes you feel happier in yourself.[3] There has been much research into the benefits of gratitude and its links to improved wellbeing. One leading gratitude researcher, Robert Emmons, found that gratitude can reduce depression and increase happiness.[4] Emmons and McCullough discovered that those who regularly journal about what they are grateful for felt better about their lives in general and they were more optimistic about their upcoming week.[5] Gratitude practice helps us to appreciate what we have and can increase the levels of satisfaction in our lives.

You can practise gratitude at any time of the day or night, and it can be as simple as thinking about one thing that you are grateful for at that time. You may be thankful for someone or something. That one thing could be something really tiny, such as someone smiling at you, a shared joke, having a breakfast you enjoy, having a hug or that it is sunny outside. It might be something bigger like something you are looking forward to at the weekend, a shared experience with a friend, a pet or something in your job. You may be grateful for a member of your family, friends, your home or your health. It does not matter what you choose to focus on; the act of practising gratitude will have a positive effect on you.

It may be helpful to get into the habit of practising gratitude at about the same point in your day so that you remember to do it. You may choose to think about what you are grateful for first thing in the morning when you wake up, or last thing before you go to sleep. It may be something you do with your family at the dinner table or friends on a shared social media or messaging site. By encouraging others to practise gratitude, you can help to raise the mood and feel-good vibes of your group. A group that shares what it is grateful for can help all its members, as one person's comment about what they are thankful for may help someone else appreciate something that they have too. By sharing the good in our lives, we help to build a positive culture. When people are struggling, it may be easier for them to share and be supported by the group.

## THINGS TO PONDER

- What are you grateful for today?

- Who or what do you appreciate today? Why?

- When might be a good time for you to practise gratitude?

# Sustainers and Drainers

There are certain things in all our lives that sustain us and make us feel good and other things that drain us. The things that drain us take our time and energy. We all have jobs, activities and responsibilities that we have to do, but not all of them bring us joy. There are, however, many things that do bring us enjoyment. It is worth thinking about the activities in your day and considering which things bring you joy, and which drain you. You are looking to achieve a balance in your day, so if you only do things that drain you, then you are going to become very tired and fed up.

Things that sustain us can be small, but they make us smile. If I were to make a list of what sustains me, I would include quality time with my family, having fun with friends, reading, writing, drawing, yoga and going for a walk in nature. I did not need to spend a long time thinking about my list, but I know if I do some of those activities or see some of those people, I will be happier.

If I consider what things I find draining, I would include ironing, report writing and trying to get my children to do their homework. All these activities need to be completed but they are not things that I look forward to doing. I find it is easier to cope with drainers if I have something that sustains me to look forward to afterwards.

It can be helpful to think about your day and what you know you need to do. What are the points in your day that will sustain you? What things in your day may drain you? Sometimes our perception of an activity may influence our opinion of it. If we can think about a positive for an otherwise draining activity then it may help us have a better experience; for example, if I need to do the ironing but I decide to watch an enjoyable TV programme at the same time, the ironing will get done but it won't feel like such a chore.

Another thing you can do is to think about your day as if it were a multilayered sandwich, where you have activities that you need to do that may drain you, but you intersperse them with activities that sustain you. I often do this if I am writing end-of-year reports, which are always time consuming. I have found that they are much easier to do if I fix a focused amount of time to write, and then do something I enjoy, such as a walk in the woods, before doing another block of report writing. This system of layering activities that we do not enjoy so much can make them more manageable. It is a way of rewarding ourselves when we have completed a task we do not enjoy by building in things that make us happy.

## THINGS TO PONDER

- What sustains you? Write a list of five things that sustain you.

- What are your drainers?

# Look for the Good

When you are busy and feel like you are going from one thing to the next without a pause it becomes harder to look for the good – to find the uplifting in the everyday. If I asked you to consider what good things you remember about today, what happened to make you smile, what would you think about? Some people find this task quite easy, and others struggle with it. Sometimes people struggle because they are looking for massive events that have brought them joy. Whereas you can find the good in the smallest of daily occurrences. It might be there was a beautiful sunrise as you drove down the hill to work, or a child offered to help pick things up when you dropped them. It could be that someone made you a cup of tea or maybe a colleague asked you about your day. Finding the good and the happiness in the small everyday things means that there is always an abundance of good to find.

The more you practise looking for the good the easier it becomes to find. You may discover that your ability to look for the positive in situations is your strength. When you make a habit of looking for the good, you may find that you feel a bit lighter, things seem a little easier and you recognize there is good around you each day.

You may also notice that you help others to look for the good in situations too. When someone is struggling or feeling negative, you may find yourself suggesting things that are good in their lives, helping them to have a subtle shift in their thoughts. This is not always appropriate to do and depends on the reasons why someone is feeling down. However, by noticing something small, such as how a colour they are wearing suits them, you can help create a small lift for them.

By looking for the good you are helping your brain to override the negative bias programmed into your mind. You start to create new pathways in your brain, as neurotransmitters fire up when you find good things in life. Your brain produces more oxytocin, which helps you feel loved and connected. Serotonin levels increase when you are satisfied and this helps you to feel secure and that you belong. You may find that you feel happier as you realize that good things are happening to you and around you all the time; sometimes you just do not see them. You may not see them because you are busy and are thinking about all the other things that you need to do, or your thoughts might be overriding a desire to look, or you may not be in the habit of looking for the good. You may need to start consciously looking for the good for it to come naturally.

When you spot good things around you, try sharing them with others; maybe ask colleagues if they saw the beautiful sunrise on the way to work that morning. You may find that you help someone else to start noticing good things around them more often. It can create a ripple effect that helps everyone to feel a bit better about themselves and their surroundings.

## THINGS TO PONDER

- What small but good things can you find today?

- Who could you share one of your good things with?

# Out in Nature

There has been much research into the benefits of going out into nature for wellbeing.[6] Even on the coldest, frostiest day being outside can help to lift our spirits and improve how we feel. Being outside often triggers our melatonin levels, which makes it easier for us to sleep at night, even if we have only been out early in the morning. Our bodies need sunlight to produce vitamin D, which helps us absorb calcium and magnesium and helps to boost our immune system. When our bodies are moving, we release endorphins that make us feel better in ourselves. Even a gentle stroll outside will give us these benefits.

When you are outside it may be the perfect time to catch up with a friend and have a walk together, which helps you feel connected. If you have had a busy week but you crave a connection with someone then a walk with them in nature may be the perfect solution. Alternatively, going for a walk on your own may make you more observant and aware of the beauty around you. Maybe you will notice birds as they sing or hop, or a ladybird crawling up a leaf. You may notice flowers that are coming into bloom or how the frost hangs on branches. You may be aware of the changing seasons and differences you see if you go out regularly.

Sometimes while walking alone, you may become caught up with the thoughts in your head. This can be a good thing if you are trying to work something through or trying to find solutions, as being outside and exercising can make it easier to process thoughts. If you have many thoughts going through your head, but you have noticed they are repetitive and unhelpful to you, walking in nature can help if you deliberately focus your attention on your surroundings. Try to focus your mind on the leaves on the trees or the shapes of the clouds in the sky. Choose to look for the beauty in your surroundings as you walk, and this may help your mind move away from repetitive thoughts. When we notice the small things around us with curiosity it helps to bring us a peacefulness and make us happy.

You can be mindful in your walking, noticing your feet as they touch the ground. Which part of your foot touches the ground first, then which part next? Consider where you feel the movement of walking in your body. Do you feel it in your ankles? Legs? Hips? Back? What does it feel like to swing your arms gently as you walk? What does it feel like to not move your arms when walking? An interesting exercise to try when you walk in nature is noticing and considering how your body feels when you move. We often take these movements for granted and do not pay them any attention. How does it feel if you move faster or slower than you usually walk? By varying the speed or route of your walk you bring a new awareness to what you are doing and your surroundings.

Mindful movement *(see page 106)* can be as simple as going for a walk in nature and bringing awareness to how your body feels during and after the walk. Having time in nature can completely change how you feel. Being outside and breathing in fresh air whilst moving your body can make you feel so much better about yourself. Being in nature can help you to notice the small, pleasant things outside. You may notice the beautiful colours of the autumn leaves as they are about to fall or the crunch of the leaves as you walk on them. Maybe you will see a bird land on a branch near you as you walk or hear its song. You may see squirrels chase each other and scamper up trees. Notice the early signs of spring, the blossom on the trees, and in winter notice the sparkling frost that makes everything appear magical. When the seasons change it is a transitional time with much to notice as nature prepares for its next phase.

When we notice the pleasant things around us, we train our minds to look for the good in little things. This attention may help us access small pockets of joy every day.

## THINGS TO PONDER

- When would you choose to walk in nature?

- How do you feel after going for a walk?

- When would be a good time to go?

# Out of Your Comfort Zone

We all have a comfort zone, a place where we feel safe and know we can happily work and manage our daily lives. We may have a comfort zone for many aspects of our lives, from how far we want to push ourselves when we exercise to conversations that we are happy to have and ones that feel more awkward. Being able to recognize our comfort zones can help us know when we are working within it and when we are pushing for more.

Think about different aspects of your life, such as relationships, exercise, diet, work, family, hobbies, spirituality and goals – what feels in your comfort zone for each area and what feels out of your comfort zone? For example, I am in my comfort zone attending a karate session, but running for 10km feels outside my comfort zone. However, there can be a middle zone, between your comfort zone and outside your comfort zone, where you can safely challenge yourself.

In your middle zone are things that you would like to do or could potentially do but they feel a bit daunting – not impossible, but they would push you. Thinking about your middle zone can be exciting – it is a new terrain that includes possible challenges for you to achieve. Having new goals and things to strive towards can be motivating and bring new vitality to your life.

You may consider which aspects of your life you would like to work on in your middle zone. It may be that you want to stretch yourself in your exercise goals or wellbeing goals, such as thinking of things you are grateful for every day for a month, or a goal of reading a book each month or completing a higher-level qualification. Whichever area you choose, applying yourself in your middle zone has the potential to enhance all areas of your life. You are positively challenging yourself to improve, and this can change many aspects of your life at the same time by shifting your perspective.

It is good to go out of our comfort zones, to feel a nervous anticipation, as this helps us to identify something that may become an accomplishment once it is achieved. In teaching we can regularly give ourselves the opportunity to stretch out of our comfort zones by teaching lessons we have not taught before, or exploring new ways of teaching. Once, I taught a class that loved Art, so I challenged myself to think of ways to add Art into different aspects of the curriculum; for example in Science by getting the children to create informative posters to explain scientific ideas. Another class I taught loved being outside, so I explored how we could incorporate more outdoor learning into our curriculum. By moving out of our comfort zones we can make our teaching more creative, which can make our classes more exciting experiences for our pupils.

## THINGS TO PONDER

- How could you venture out of your comfort zone?

- How could you explore coming out of your comfort zone in different aspects of your life?

- What could be your first small step?

# Trust Your Intuition

We all have a natural gauge built into us that helps to protect us when we do not feel safe. Our bodies do different things to alert us if something does not feel right. It may be a funny feeling or a strong desire to do something or not to do something. This is our intuition and it's there to protect us. You may find you have a feeling of dread, a pulling feeling in your stomach or something else that is your warning sign.

Learning to trust our intuition is important, and as a teacher, it may be the first thing that alerts us when things do not feel right. Sometimes we have those intuitive feelings when we first step out of our comfort zone, and we are not sure if it is going to be okay to try something new. On the occasions when we know that we are pushing out of our comfort zone it is good to recognize what signals your body sends to you when it is starting to feel unsafe.

Some people are not tuned in to their body and the signals that it sends – they have spent years ignoring what their body is telling them. Their body then needs to make bigger gestures, like making them ill to get them to stop. You can start tuning in to the signals that your body sends at any time. All you need to do is pause when you are asked to do something out of your comfort zone and see how your body responds.

Your intuition is there to protect you and those you love. It is our own natural gauge that lets us know when things do not feel safe. Listen to your intuition by tuning in to your body and recognizing the messages that your body is sending you. It is helpful to know what triggers are in your body. You might find it helpful to tune in to your body for a few days and see what you notice when different situations arise. Do you feel anything in your body at different times? For example, if you are walking to the car and it is dark and quiet, what do you notice in your body? Or if you are approached by a parent, what do you feel in your body? What do you think about at these times? Our intuition is based on perceived dangers that we have envisioned in our minds, or responses to things that have happened to us or what we have been told. All this information becomes our perception, and this affects our intuition. Tuning in to the reactions from our body helps us to recognize any real or perceived dangers and what does not feel right to us for whatever reason.

As teachers, we need to safeguard the children in our care, and often it is our intuition that alerts us to a concern about a child or their circumstance. You may notice small changes in the child, or you may pick up on things that they say. You may start to notice patterns in behaviour that worry you or changes in communication from the child or their family. When you notice these things, it is important to report them, even if they seem small in isolation. Sometimes an accumulation of small incidents or perceptions can help to form a larger picture. Sometimes it is that you have noticed a one-off incident or occurrence. It is always best to report concerns, however small. Your school will have a lead for safeguarding – in England this person would be called the Designated Safeguard Lead (DSL) – whom you should speak to if you have any queries or concerns, as well as recording them in the school record-keeping system. Each school has their own recording system, so if you are new to the school or unsure of its recording system, ask to be shown how to use it.

You may speak to the parents or carers of the pupil about any concerns that you have regarding what you have noticed. It may be that you can offer the family support by guiding them towards other systems the school has in place to help them. In addition, these conversations may help you understand whether you are dealing with a one-off incident or something that the family are struggling with in the long term.

- When have you felt things are not right?

- What do you do when you notice your intuition has sensed something?

## Comparison and Being Unique

When you first start teaching, when you move to a new school or get a new leadership team, you may feel that you need to prove yourself. You may feel pressure to show that you are good at your job and that you are a worthy teacher in the school. This pressure comes from within us, rather than being imposed on us by others. We have this inner desire to be liked, respected and acknowledged. This is something that we have little control over; however, by being aware that these thoughts are often just thoughts, not facts, then they can start to lose some of their power. When we recognize that it is our own thoughts that are making us compare ourselves to others and feel like we need to prove our worth, then our thoughts have less control.

The old saying that 'comparison is the thief of joy', often attributed to Theodore Roosevelt, has lots of truth in it. We are all unique individuals with different backgrounds, experiences and personalities, so it is impossible for us to compare ourselves to others because we know that we are not the same. When we look at others and see things that we consider they may do better than us – or we think they are more popular, a better teacher, have better dress sense, are more confident than us – we do not do anything to help ourselves. These thoughts and opinions about others are not facts and comparing ourselves to others becomes a way of diminishing ourselves. It becomes a way of putting ourselves down, which is only going to make us feel bad.

Rather than comparing yourself to others, consider what you admire about another person and what they might admire about you. Think about what you are good at and what you take pride in. I think it is great that children learn from a range of unique, individual teachers. The children in your class get to experience what you are passionate about and what ignites you. Then, when they have a different teacher, they'll learn about the unique characteristics of that teacher. This helps children to learn and thrive in different ways. To start with it helps them understand that we are all different and we all have qualities to celebrate and not everyone's qualities are the same. How empowering it is for a child to sit in an assembly hall and look around at the teachers who are role modelling how great it is to be yourself and celebrate that. It also helps children to explore what they like and what they enjoy; it helps them know it is okay to be themselves.

If we start to celebrate what we are all great at then we can help to raise each other up, rather than comparing ourselves to others, diminishing our uniqueness. There is no need for comparison and feeling you need to prove yourself if you are being authentically yourself and trying your best. That does not mean that you need to be always 100 per cent your best self, as that is not possible. It is about being true to yourself. It is okay to have a bad day or to find things difficult. This is what we would encourage the children in our classes to recognize – that we do not have to be perfect to be liked and respected, we just need to be ourselves.

## THINGS TO PONDER

- When are you most likely to doubt yourself or compare yourself to others?

- What do you admire in others?

- What unique gifts do you have?

- How do you celebrate yourself?

# PART III

# Tapping

# CHAPTER 7

# Introduction to Tapping

*'Under chronic stress, your body is
more apt to enter a state of dis-ease.
Unable to achieve its natural balance,
it can't function the way it should.'*

NICK ORTNER

Tapping is a brilliant practice to help you feel more relaxed and in control of your choices. It is also known as the Emotional Freedom Technique (EFT). When you tap it gives you the power to acknowledge, work with and regulate your feelings. Tapping helps to reduce the effects of cortisol and adrenaline on the body when it is stressed. It is a quick and easy technique to learn and you can even use it when you only have a minute or two to reset yourself. Once you have learned how to tap, you can use it for many different stressors and symptoms.

## What Is Tapping?

Tapping is a powerful technique that lowers the level of cortisol, known as the stress hormone, in the body. During the practice, you gently tap on points of your body to send calming signals to your brain. At the same time, you express how you are feeling with statements you say to yourself either in your mind or out loud. There are nine main tapping points situated across the face and body: on the side of the hand (the karate-chop point), the eyebrow, the side of the eye, under the eye, under the nose, the chin, the collarbone, underarm and the top of the head. All of the points are easily accessible for children and adults to tap on by themselves.

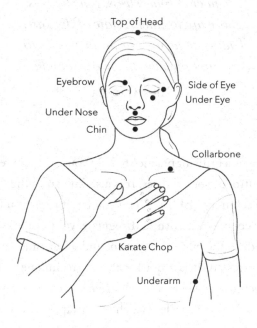

*EFT Tapping Points*

Before we start tapping, we think about what we want to work on and give the issue a rating on a scale of zero to 10, where 10 expresses the worst something could possibly be and zero is the least impact it has on us. At the end of a sequence of a few tapping rounds, we give another scaled rating to compare how we feel.

We start tapping on the side of the hand at the karate-chop point by saying how we are feeling at that time – this may be a physical or emotional feeling. For example we may say, 'Even though I am feeling overwhelmed by the amount of work I need to do, I love and accept myself'. This is known as the set-up statement. We try to accept how we are feeling by saying, 'I love and accept myself.' It is sometimes difficult to say these words; if so try replacing them with 'I'm okay' or 'I accept my feelings.' We repeat the set-up statement three times while tapping on the side of one hand before moving on to tap on the other main points – the eyebrow, the side of the eye, under the eye, under the nose, the chin, the collarbone, underarm and the top of the head. On each of these eight subsequent points we make our statement once about how we are feeling or what we are thinking.

You can choose to tap using one or both hands, tapping on each point using two or three fingers to gently tap six to eight times on each point. If you choose to tap using both hands then you can tap both eyebrows, side of eyes, under eyes, collarbones, underarms and use both hands to tap the top of the head. Due to the small space under your nose and chin it is often easier to tap there with one hand. It does not matter which hand you use to tap or which side of the body you choose to tap if you are tapping with one hand.

# The Benefits of Tapping

Tapping may be described as a stress management technique or a relaxation skill, as it has an effect on the body and brain. Tapping is similar to acupuncture, but without needles, because you stimulate different points on your body to release tension. By following the tapping sequence and stating your issue, you are acknowledging your feelings, while sending calming signals to your brain indicating that you are safe in that moment.

Tapping is effective in relieving anxiety, depression, physical pain, phobias, worries, trauma and limiting beliefs. It has been scientifically proven to reduce stress, lower cortisol levels, improve sleep, reduce anxiety and increase productivity. Tapping calms the part of the brain that is responsible for triggering a stress response. Repeated tapping practices help to create new neural pathways in the brain to help you feel less triggered in the future.

There are many benefits of tapping, but I think one of the most powerful things is how quickly it helps. The power of tapping continues to amaze me. It is something that is so accessible to people that once they have learned how to do it, they have a strategy that they can use whenever necessary. Tapping does not need to cost any money but can make a huge difference. When you tap and say the things that are worrying you, you take the power out of the worries as you let your body know you are safe. You lower your levels of stress by acknowledging how you are feeling. The tapping action itself helps to make you feel calmer and supports the lowering of stress hormones in your body.

When we are stressed our cortisol levels rise and our body thinks that it is unsafe and needs to be protected. Our stress levels can rise for a number of reasons – it may be something as small as running late when we want to get somewhere on time; this can make us agitated or short-tempered and it can affect our thought processes. We may be triggered by many of these low-level stressors every day, such as if someone drives aggressively, if we forget to do something we said we would do, when our child is upset, if someone is rude to us and many other things that can happen. Each time these stressors occur our cortisol levels may rise, and we can feel the effects of stress in our bodies.

When we notice we are feeling stress in our body, we can lower that stress and cortisol level by tapping. When you tap you are sending calming signals to the brain. You can tap at any time and feel calmer and more in control within minutes. The more specific you can be about what is causing you stress, the easier it is to access how you are feeling at that time. For example, if you need to leave home early for work, but your teenage child still hasn't got into the shower, it would be easy to get cross quickly – by pausing for a couple of minutes and tapping on the frustration you are feeling, you will become calmer so that you approach the situation in a more controlled way. In this situation, you could tap saying phrases such as, 'I feel so frustrated; I do not want to be late; I do not want to rush.' You cannot say the wrong thing when you are tapping; just express your thoughts and feelings as you tap, and it helps you to feel less stressed.

I think that one of the main benefits of tapping is having an easy tool that you can use whenever you wish; it is free, always available and has the ability to make you feel better in minutes. If there was an advert to promote tapping, you would think it would come with a high price tag as the benefits are huge. I would love tapping to be a tool that is widely used in education for all parties – children, teachers, parents and school leaders – as it is something that helps everyone to regulate themselves, express themselves and feel in control of their actions. It is so easy to do once you have learned the basic tapping points. You can use tapping anytime and

I use it to feel better in many situations or to have more clarity in my thinking.

# How Does Tapping Work?

Our levels of stress can affect how we sleep and change how we react to and experience life. Stress has been proven to be a huge contributing factor to our overall health and wellbeing. We are more likely to get ill, and take longer to recover from being ill, if we are stressed. Stress can come from so many aspects of our lives that it can be hard to pinpoint a cause. We may have worries about health, money, our families, work and so many other areas in our lives.

The amygdala is an ancient part of the human brain that produces the stress hormone cortisol. It helps to keep us safe when we perceive danger. For our early ancestors, this meant initiating a quick fight-or-flight response when faced with an immediate danger, such as a possible attack by a predator. Often, in modern society, our cortisol levels are raised when we have worries such as a looming deadline, an interview or an important meeting. Our body's natural reaction is to identify these worries as threats. Our amygdala is like the guard dog to our brain – it is there to protect us. Sometimes our amygdala guard dog barks and tries to keep us safe when we are not in danger but we do not feel comfortable in a situation.

The prefrontal cortex, at the front of our brain, helps us with our rational thinking. It is not fully developed until we reach our mid-20s; even when it has developed, if our amygdala signals that we are not safe, our prefrontal cortex struggles to react rationally. Although our prefrontal cortex helps us to make rational decisions, our amygdala may override it by producing more cortisol when we do not feel safe. This is where tapping can be useful, as it helps to reduce the amount of cortisol being produced by the amygdala, allowing us to feel calmer and to think more rationally and clearly. As we tap, we acknowledge and recognize the fears and worries that we are experiencing or the physical symptoms we are feeling, and saying them out loud decreases their hold over us.

Tapping lowers stress hormone levels and lets the body and brain know it is safe to relax and approach a situation calmly. Often when we are triggered, we do not feel safe. Our bodies go into fight, flight or freeze mode. This state can be caused by both real and perceived dangers. When we do not feel safe, our bodies produce more adrenaline and cortisol. The adrenaline helps us to move quickly away from danger, as threats to our ancient ancestors would have been physical, such as being chased by a predator. When our body is flooded with adrenaline our blood is redirected to our muscles, enabling us to move fast, but it is taken away from our organs, putting them under strain. As discussed in Chapter 4 *(see page 89)*, when we are in a fight, flight or freeze mode it is harder for us to make decisions; we act in survival mode. Nowadays, our perceived threats may come from an email or a conversation that makes us feel threatened or judged. We cannot help how our bodies respond when we do not feel safe, but we can use strategies such as mindfulness and tapping to help us feel more grounded and calmer, and this helps us to question if threats are real or perceived.

When we are stressed, we have a choice – we can choose to react by setting ourselves into fight, flight or freeze mode, or we can choose to respond and feel more in control of our stress. Tapping and mindfulness offer us the choice of whether we want to react or respond. Both practices incorporate strategies that help to calm our minds and our thoughts, allowing us to decide how we want to behave or what we want to do. When we tap, we are able to access memories in our subconscious mind – allowing us to deal with the root cause of our concerns or fears. This is partly why tapping is such an effective tool.

## The History of Tapping

In 1980, Dr Roger Callahan, an American psychologist, created individual algorithms of tapping for specific issues. His work was developed further by one of his trainees, Gary Craig, in the 1990s. Gary Craig evolved his theory and simplified the tapping sequence to create the Emotional Freedom Technique (EFT), the method we still use today. Tapping was initially used to help soldiers who were suffering from post-traumatic stress disorder (PTSD). Some of these soldiers were unable to sleep, had harrowing flashbacks and their whole lives were impacted. Tapping helped with the effects of PTSD with lasting results.[1]

Further research found that tapping helped with many other mental, emotional and physical symptoms by calming the nervous system. As we mentioned earlier, our bodies do all kinds of amazing things to protect us and keep us safe, from giving us physical pain to causing anxiety and panic attacks. When we calm the nervous system with tapping, we support our bodies and minds.

In recent years, more positive psychology has been applied to tapping, where it is introduced after acknowledging and working through negative thoughts, feelings and emotions. Tapping has become more widely recognized and is now on the

National Institute for Health Excellence (NICE) list in the UK of evidence-based treatments that doctors can recommend.[2] Recently, tapping has been promoted by celebrities, including Fearne Cotton and Lily Allen, as something that they use either for specific issues or as a self-regulation technique.

Now, decades of research has proved that tapping can help with issues of anxiety, worry, depression, PTSD, as well as pain, weight loss and phobias.[3] This work is ongoing and there are new findings emerging from countries around the world every year.

## Tapping for Worries

Worrying has a negative impact on us; we worry about things that are coming up or things that we think could happen. As we worry, our minds are busy with similar thoughts going round and round, and we may feel hijacked by them. Tapping can help us to notice how we are feeling and recognize the thoughts we are having, which quite often are negative or full of worry. Often, when we get stuck in a loop of worrying thoughts circling, we are unable to find solutions to our problems. You may have noticed that you arrive at solutions or helpful ideas when you are out walking, or in the shower. At these times, our minds are more relaxed and therefore able to problem-solve. Tapping can have a similar effect as it helps us to feel calmer and safer in our minds and bodies so we can think more clearly, or the worry dissipates. When we give our minds a break for a moment then we become more creative in our ideas.

We can tap whenever we notice that we are worrying about something. Often, as our thoughts are repetitive, we may have been worrying about the same thing for some time before we register it. As you tap through the tapping points you say how you are feeling and the thoughts you are thinking – this will help you express the worry, recognize how it is making you feel and reduce the hold that the worry has on you. The tapping process helps to reduce the charge of the worry, making it more neutral.

We start by tapping on the negative, on all the worries, thoughts and feelings we are experiencing. By tapping on the negative we are acknowledging what is there, safely allowing us to express ourselves while sending calming signals to our brain. As we tap, our brain reduces the level of cortisol that it produces when we are stressed. We can then consider our worrying thoughts more calmly. It may be that we recognize that we are worrying about something in the future that might not even happen, we have perceived a threat that might not be there.

As teachers, we can become overloaded with information, which comes at us all the time and from different directions. While teaching, we are constantly monitoring and checking the pupils in our class, helping them learn and supporting them when they have problems outside school. We have information from parents in person, through emails, phone calls or via the school administration team. We also have information from colleagues, senior leaders and external agencies. All these different people and sources of information, all needing attention and focus. We can become saturated and our brains can find it hard to focus on one thing, while we try to juggle everything. I find that I am at my least productive when I feel saturated with information, as my brain is overloaded. When this happens, I need to slow down and take a moment to pause.

Research by the psychologist Mihaly Csikszentmihalyi has shown that when we try to multitask, our productivity can reduce by as much as 30 per cent.[4] Our brains are better focusing on one thing, then taking our attention to the next thing. When we chop and change between tasks, we often do each task less well than if we did one at a time. While teaching a class, it may be difficult or even impossible to focus on one task. There are things that we can do to help us focus though, such as not checking emails while teaching pupils in a class, unless it is absolutely necessary. It can help to clump tasks together, to have one focus at a time and give our brains less to remember; for example, decide on a set time each week when you are going to plan lessons and another time when you are going to produce resources.

When we have so much that needs our attention, it can be overwhelming, and we can feel unsure about where to start. We can focus our minds by tapping, by pausing and slowing down to think more clearly.

## How Can I Use Tapping in My Life?

Tapping is a tool that we can use as often as we like to feel calmer and more in control of our lives. Worries and concerns can take over our thought processes and affect our actions. By using tapping we can take the 'charge' out of the worry so that we can make better choices and feel calmer.

If you are in a situation where you think it would be beneficial to tap but you do not want to tap in public, I have found that visualizing that you are tapping on each point whilst thinking about what you want to focus on can really help. For example, imagine tapping on each point and thinking, 'I'm so tired' or 'There are too many thoughts in my head'. You can do as many rounds of this as you find useful. Visualizing tapping on the points can also be useful if you want to tap in the night as you will not disturb anyone who shares your room or bed. There are tapping scripts in this book that you can use before going to bed or when waking in the night *(see page 183)*.

## How Can Tapping Help Teachers?

We may feel fine and think we are coping and managing well, then the smallest of things can make everything feel too much. We may then become negative about ourselves, blaming ourselves for not being able to maintain this constant juggling. Tapping can help us to pause, acknowledge how we are feeling, help us feel calmer and think more clearly.

As tapping does not take long to do, you can tap for a few minutes at breaktime to feel more composed. I have had times when I know that I am working really hard, but then I've received an email from a parent that feels accusatory and questions the decisions I've made. In these instances, where I know that I need to speak to the parent, I will always do so face to face or by phone rather than email, which can be misinterpreted. When you speak to someone, they feel heard, you can listen to their concerns and they can hear that you are genuine when you speak to them. When possible, I will tap before making a phone call or speaking to the parent so that I feel calm and collected before our conversation.

I find that it is useful to tap if I am finding a child's behaviour challenging; if I have tapped, I will be calmer and will make more-considered choices about how to respond to the child, rather than be aggravated by their behaviour and react in a way that I may not otherwise choose. In situations like this, discreetly tapping on the finger points is really useful as no one needs to see the small movements on your hand. To tap on the finger points, use your thumb to tap on the side of the nail of each finger on the same hand. Tap a few times on each finger before moving on to the next one. You can use your index finger to go over the top of your thumb to tap on the other side of your thumbnail.

If you have a family and want to give them the best of you when you return home, rather than what is left over after you have taught for the day, then it is well worth tapping before leaving the school car park or before entering your home. By taking a few minutes to tap, you are calming your nervous system and letting go of things that may be bothering you about the day. You can even tap and say how tired you are feeling and by the time you have finished tapping, you should feel more energized. I think the guilt of being a teacher and a parent can be huge, because you may feel that the children you teach get the best of you and your own children get the remainder. By investing in yourself and tapping for a few moments, that balance can shift so that you have less guilt and can give your children your full focus. They can then benefit from more quality time with you.

## Tapping Alone or with a Practitioner

In this book, you will find a number of tapping scripts that you can follow along to, tapping on the points on your body and either saying the script aloud or in your head. It is important that before you start tapping, you consider what number on a zero to 10 scale you are on. When you have completed two or three rounds of tapping on the main nine points, you should check your scaled number again. This scaling will help you assess how you are feeling and whether you need to continue to tap. Generally, you should continue tapping if your score is higher than three or if you feel that you need to tap for longer.

If you visit a tapping practitioner for a session, they would look closely to see how you are responding during the process to decide how many rounds of tapping would be beneficial for you. They would notice if you become more agitated or if your skin flushes or pales in response, as well as verbally checking in with you. A tapping practitioner would ask questions to tailor the tapping to what you need. They are likely to use different scripts and wording each time they tap with you as they will be responding to what you share with them. Also, they may guide you through many rounds of tapping, developing and refining what you are tapping on. They may also use extra tapping points to the nine in this book, depending on what you would like to work on with them.

With a tapping practitioner, you can work on traumas, anxieties, phobias and specific areas of pain or distress. They will be able to discuss your issues and tap through them. Many concerns can be addressed in a few sessions.

The generic tapping scripts in this book cover many issues that you can work through yourself. If you find that one of the phrases does not feel right for you, repeat a previous phrase that does feel right. The more you tap the more intuitive you are likely to become, meaning you may be less reliant on scripts, or you may do the first round following a script and then do the next round using phrases that feel right for you.

Tapping helps you access your subconscious, which contains all your old memories and perceptions about what you have experienced. We do not have control over our subconscious, but it affects how we react and respond in different situations. My brother and I had the same childhood experiences, but we remember things about our childhood differently. This is partly because I am two years older than him so I have a different interpretation of events; partly because we felt different things during our childhood that would shape our memories; and partly because we are different people with different perspectives. How we experience the world is unique to us, so even if you have a shared experience with someone, they may have different memories to you about that experience. It is part of what makes us all unique: We bring our own past experiences, emotions and beliefs to any situation and that moulds our new experiences.

We can state our thoughts, emotions and beliefs while we tap on the tapping points around the body. Whilst we tap and say things, we allow ourselves to acknowledge them in that moment. The tapping helps to calm our nervous system making us feel safer to express what we are thinking at that time. As we tap, we help our brain to create new, positive neural pathways. The more you tap the stronger these pathways become. In this way, if you work with a tapping practitioner, you can work on challenging situations from your past to help reduce the charge or power that they may hold over you.

Tapping helps to calm the nervous system. It is quick and easy to do and can help you feel calmer in minutes. I think tapping is a useful tool for anyone to use at any time. Just tapping around the points, without even saying anything, will calm your nerves. When I first introduce tapping to someone, I show them the main tapping points and ask them to copy where I tap to help them learn the points. Sometimes, when someone is very stressed or anxious, just tapping around the points helps them feel calm enough to share how they are feeling. The act of tapping, even without saying anything, can help them to calm down and regulate.

## Tapping in School

In schools, tapping can help staff cope with personal issues, as well as feel calmer in moments of stress. It can help children with self-regulation and may be used as a way of getting a group of children's attention.

I often use tapping in my class to draw the children together when they are excited, and I need them to focus on the next instruction or task. I say to the class, 'Everyone do this' while tapping on the top of my head and they all copy and then switch to tap on the collarbone or another tapping point. Even doing this for 30 seconds changes the energy in the class quickly. Everyone is focused on copying what I am doing, and they also have their hands busy whilst calming their nervous system. It is one of the best methods I have found for getting children's attention and calming them down. I have used tapping in this way when leading a whole-school assembly and the children have become excited about something we have done. Tapping quickly calms the whole assembly hall without any voices being raised.

Recently, I was taking a group of Year 6 students for a series of sessions to help them feel more confident in their Maths and English, ready for the standardized tests that children in England need to complete in their last year of primary school. I started by asking the children what they wanted to work on during our sessions together. One child said that she gets incredibly nervous before tests and asked if we could do anything to help with that. Other children in the group echoed what she was saying. I told them that I could teach them breathing techniques and that I could teach them how to tap.

To start with, I just taught them the tapping points – we did not say any statements or scale our feelings, we just tapped on the main tapping points for a couple of rounds. In this short time, some of them reflected how they felt more relaxed already and asked to do more. Later that day, their class teacher came to tell me that she had seen a couple of boys tapping and asked them about it. One boy who had been in my group shared how he had learned how to tap that day and that it had helped him so much that he wanted to teach his friends so they could feel better too. A girl in the group had gone home to find her sister was upset, so she taught her the tapping technique she had learned to help her sister. This example shows how powerful tapping can be at helping you to regulate your emotions; you do not need to be a tapping expert to feel the benefits of tapping.

# CHAPTER 8

# Tapping for Life

*'Self-sabotage is simply misguided self-love.'*

BRAD YATES

W e all experience times when we feel our stress levels rise, when things start to get on top of us. Whether you are not sleeping well, having panic attacks, holding tension in your body or you are feeling anxious, tapping may help you regulate yourself and feel more in control. This chapter is divided into short sections, each covering a different everyday situation and including a dedicated tapping script. I have produced videos for some of these tapping scripts, which you can find on my YouTube channel and website *(see page 231)*. Audio recordings can also be found in the audiobook, which is available in the *Empower You Unlimited Audio* app *(see page 233)* or wherever you listen to your audiobooks.

## Tension in the Body

When we are stressed, worried or anxious we hold tension in our bodies. We may walk around with our shoulders hunched up or our fists clenched tight. We may feel tension in our stomach or neck.

It may be that we are even tense when in bed, grinding or clenching our teeth. This tension makes it hard for us to relax and focus.

# TAPPING SCRIPT

- Before starting this tapping practice, we are going to scan our bodies and see where we feel the tension.

- Sit in a comfortable position with your feet flat on the floor and your hands resting on your thighs. Roll your shoulders and relax your neck.

- Take a few deep breaths and with each exhalation feel yourself relax further.

- Start to scan your body by taking all your attention to your feet. Focus on the soles of your feet, then your toes, your heels and the tops of your feet.

- Move your attention to your ankles, your calves and lower legs, your knees and your thighs.

- Move your awareness to your stomach and pelvis. Then to your lower back, middle back and top of your back.

- Think about your arms: your upper arms, elbows, lower arms, wrists, the backs of your hands, fingers and palms of your hands.

- Move your attention to your shoulders, neck, back of your head, crown of your head and forehead. Then to your ears, eyebrows, space between your eyebrows, eyes, nose, cheeks, lips and chin.

Find where you have tension or unease in your body. Rate your tension points from zero to 10, with 10 being the most amount of tension and zero being the least amount.

Start tapping on the side of your hand, saying the statements at each point; note that the side of hand point is repeated three times.

## Round One

> *Side of hand: Even though I have this tension in my body, I am okay and accept myself.*
>
> *Side of hand: Even though I have this tension in my body, I am okay and accept myself.*
>
> *Side of hand: Even though I have this tension in my body, I am okay and accept myself.*
>
> *Eyebrow: This tension in my body.*
>
> *Side of eye: This tension in my body.*
>
> *Under eye: This tension in my body.*
>
> *Under nose: This tension in my body.*
>
> *Chin: This tension in my body.*
>
> *Collarbone: This tension in my body.*
>
> *Underarm: This tension in my body.*
>
> *Top of head: This tension in my body.*

## Round Two

In this round, begin by thinking about the tension precisely using the guided thoughts below, then, from the chin point, say the statements describing your tension aloud.

> *Eyebrow: Think about the tension in your body. What colour is it?*
>
> *Side of eye: Think about what shape it is.*
>
> *Under eye: Think about the texture of the tension. Is it spiky, smooth or rough?*

*Under nose: Think about how it feels. Is it sticky, fluid or hard?*

*Chin: This* (say colour) *tension.*

*Collarbone: This* (say shape) *tension.*

*Underarm: This* (say texture) *tension.*

*Top of head: The* (say feeling) *of this tension.*

## Round Three

*Eyebrow: Think about the tension in your body. What colour is it?*

*Side of eye: Think about what shape it is.*

*Under eye: Think about the texture of the tension. Is it spiky, smooth or rough?*

*Under nose: Think about how it feels. Is it sticky, fluid or hard?*

*Chin: This tension in my body.*

*Collarbone: This tension in my body.*

*Underarm: This tension in my body.*

*Top of head: This tension in my body.*

Take a deep breath in and out. Rate your tension on a scale of zero to 10. By bringing awareness to where we experience tension in our body and then feeling into it as we tap, we can ease the tension. You may wish to follow this tapping script more than once if you still have remaining tension in your body. Sometimes it may feel like the tension is moving around your body as you may have noticed tension in one place, then as you tap that tension subsides and you feel tension somewhere else. If this happens, keep tapping on the different places you feel tension in your body.

· · · · · · · · · · · · · · · · · · · · · · · · ·

# Tension in Your Teeth

This script will help you if you know that you either grind your teeth or clench your jaw. If you do this at night, you may have jaw pain in the morning, or your dentist may have mentioned that you have signs of trauma in your teeth. It is good to recognize that you have this ongoing pain or tension and that it is likely to be stress-related. Tapping can reduce the stress and the tension in your body, therefore reducing the amount you grind or clench your teeth.

## TAPPING SCRIPT

Start by taking a deep breath in and out. Rate on a zero to 10 scale the amount of tension or pain that you have in your jaw, with 10 being the most amount of tension or pain. We're going to start by tapping on the side of the hand. Gently breathe and just repeat the words below in your mind or out loud.

### Round One

*Side of hand: Even though I know that I am clenching my teeth, I deeply love and accept myself.*

*Side of hand: Even though I know that my jaw is sore because of what I do to my teeth at night, I deeply love and accept myself.*

*Side of hand: Even though I grind my teeth and clench my jaw when I'm asleep, I deeply love and accept myself.*

*Eyebrow: I clench my teeth.*

*Side of eye: I grind my teeth.*

*Under eye: My whole jaw feels tight.*

*Under nose: I have tension in my jaw.*

*Chin: Tension from my day gets processed at night.*

*Collarbone: All this tension in my body.*

*Underarm: All this tension.*

*Top of head: I hold this tension in my jaw.*

## Round Two

*Eyebrow: This is something that I cannot control.*

*Side of eye: This is something that's been happening for a long time.*

*Under eye: I know that I'm doing it.*

*Under nose: I know that it's happening.*

*Chin: But I am powerless to stop.*

*Collarbone: All this tension in my body.*

*Underarm: All this tension in my jaw.*

*Top of head: I feel this tension.*

## Round Three

*Eyebrow: I choose to relax my jaw.*

*Side of eye: I choose to relax my tongue.*

*Under eye: I choose to relax my teeth.*

*Under nose: I choose for my chin to relax.*

*Chin: I choose for my gums to feel relaxed.*

*Collarbone: I choose my whole jaw to be relaxed.*

*Underarm: I choose my whole jaw to be relaxed.*

*Top of head: I choose my jaw to be relaxed.*

Gently stop tapping. Take a deep breath in. Rate how much tension is now in your jaw on a zero to 10 scale; hopefully, your scaled score has reduced. If it is still higher than you would like, then repeat the tapping practice. By doing this practice regularly, the message you are sending to your body is that it is okay to relax. It is safe to relax. You are recognizing what is going on in your body, but also, you would like it to relax.

. . . . . . . . . . . . . . . . . . . . . . . . .

# When You Can't Focus

Let's think about our ability to focus. Sometimes we find it hard to focus and our mind wanders to all the things that we need to do: bills we need to pay, emails we need to answer and things we need to do at home like organizing dinners and supporting our family. All of these things can make us feel overwhelmed and make it hard for us to focus.

## TAPPING SCRIPT

I would like you to think about what a lack of focus feels like for you. Maybe you feel overwhelmed by everything you have to do. Maybe there's a frustration around focusing. When you think about it, I would like you to rate your feelings about focusing on a scale of zero to 10, with 10 meaning you are completely overwhelmed and unable to focus and zero meaning that you are feeling fine.

We are going to take a deep breath in and start tapping on the karate-chop point on the side of the hand. Say the words either in your mind or aloud.

## Round One

*Side of hand: Even though I'm struggling to focus, I acknowledge how I feel and I give my body permission to relax.*

*Side of hand: Even though life can be overwhelming and impacts my focus, I acknowledge how hard it has been and I give my mind permission to relax.*

*Side of hand: Even though I find it hard to focus, and there is so much going on, I'm open to new ideas as I allow my mind and body to relax.*

*Eyebrow: This lack of focus.*

*Side of eye: I worry about my lack of focus.*

*Under eye: I have a lot to contend with.*

*Under nose: I have a lot of responsibility.*

*Chin: I have so much to do.*

*Collarbone: I feel like I need to do it all.*

*Underarm: I don't want to miss out or let anyone down.*

*Top of head: Trying to do it all at once.*

## Round Two

*Eyebrow: It is exhausting.*

*Side of eye: It is overwhelming.*

*Under eye: I am so distracted.*

*Under nose: I often blame myself.*

*Chin: I want to be better at focusing.*

*Collarbone: But my brain is not working that way.*

*Underarm: I want to be better at focusing.*

*Top of head: But it feels so hard to do.*

## Round Three

*Eyebrow: I let my body relax more and more.*

*Side of eye: Feeling grounded and centred.*

*Under eye: I'm ready to release this overwhelm.*

*Under nose: It's not making me feel good.*

*Chin: I don't need to do everything at once.*

*Collarbone: I do not need all the answers.*

*Underarm: I give myself permission to release this.*

*Top of head: It's safe to take a break.*

## Round Four

*Eyebrow: It is safe to protect my mind.*

*Side of eye: By releasing distraction.*

*Under eye: I might not have all the answers.*

*Under nose: I still have things on my to-do list.*

*Chin: I can relax and still be focused.*

*Collarbone: I can relax and be focused, right here and right now.*

*Underarm: I am enough.*

*Top of head: I can take a break and feel calm. Calm and centred in my body.*

I would like you to gently stop tapping and take a breath; take a deep breath in your own time. I would like you to think about the ability to focus and how overwhelmed you may be feeling about all the other things you have to do. Rate that feeling again on a zero to 10 scale, with 10 meaning that you are completely overwhelmed, and it feels impossible to focus, and zero meaning that you feel much calmer and you are able to focus. I hope this has helped you to feel more focused.

. . . . . . . . . . . . . . . . . . . . . .

# When You Have Too Much to Do

There may be times in the week when you feel like there is too much to do, when everything feels overwhelming. There may be lots going on in your home life and in school, and it can all feel too much. Tapping can really help when you feel like this because it gives you time to pause, to stop and to recognize how you are feeling in your body and then, hopefully, be able to see a different way forward.

## TAPPING SCRIPT

Before you start tapping, I would like you to rate on a scale of zero to 10 how intensely you feel there is too much going on at the moment. A score of 10 means that the most amount is going on and zero means that everything is fine and that you can cope.

Take a deep breath in and out. Start tapping on the side of your hand and repeat this point three times. You can say the phrases aloud or in your head as you continue to tap.

## Round One

> *Side of hand: Even though I've got so much going on and it all feels too much, I accept myself and how I am feeling.*

> *Side of hand: Even though I've got so much going on and it all feels too much, I accept myself and how I am feeling.*

> *Side of hand: Even though I've got so much going on and it all feels too much, I accept myself and how I am feeling.*

> *Eyebrow: So much going on.*

> *Side of eye: There's so much going on at the moment.*

> *Under eye: Making me feel overwhelmed.*

> *Under nose: Feeling overwhelmed by how much is going on.*

> *Chin: Too much to do.*

> *Collarbone: Too much to think about.*

> *Underarm: Not getting to stop.*

> *Top of head: It was hard to take a break.*

## Round Two

> *Eyebrow: So much to do.*

> *Side of eye: I don't know how to change it.*

> *Under eye: It's been like this for a while.*

> *Under nose: Too much going on.*

> *Chin: This feeling of overwhelm.*

> *Collarbone: Do I feel it in my stomach?*

> *Underarm: Do I feel tension in my chest or shoulders?*

> *Top of head: Have I been clenching my jaw?*

## Round Three

*Eyebrow: Do I feel a bit chaotic?*

*Side of eye: Thinking about what I am feeling right now in my body.*

*Under eye: So much going on.*

*Under nose: It's good to pause.*

*Chin: To give myself time to think.*

*Collarbone: All these things are going on.*

*Underarm: So much going on.*

*Top of head: But I choose to pause and recognize what's going on in my body.*

When you are ready, gently stop tapping and take a deep breath in and out. Whilst taking a deep breath, think again about that zero to 10 scale. What are you feeling right now? Ten on the scale means that everything still feels overwhelming, and zero means everything is completely fine.

. . . . . . . . . . . . . . . . . . . . . . .

Hopefully, you will have gone down the scale and you feel that you have a little more control and your mind is not quite so busy. Well done for taking time out for yourself. By stopping and giving yourself five minutes to tap and recognize what is going on in your body, you have acknowledged how you are feeling and it will be easier to find a way through everything you need to do. It can be helpful after doing this tapping session to write down the top one or two things that you need to do. Often if we complete the most pressing tasks, the others do not feel so significant and overwhelming.

# Difficulty Sleeping

Sleep is a basic human need. We need to sleep in order to function and be at our best. When our sleep is broken or when we have difficulty either getting to sleep or staying asleep then it can affect us in many ways. Lack of sleep can affect how well we process information and make choices for our health, such as eating healthy food or finding the energy to exercise. Sleep can even affect our weight. One of the most noticeable differences can be changes in our mood and how we react to situations. While we sleep, we process what has happened during the day and our body rests, recharges and repairs itself.

It is easy to worry when we have difficulty getting to sleep because we know that if we do not sleep it may affect us the next day. The more stressed we get about sleep, the harder it is to fall asleep. The more relaxed we feel when we go to bed, the easier it will be to fall asleep. Tapping can help us to reduce stress levels and therefore make it easier to sleep.

## TAPPING SCRIPT

Before you start to tap, find a calm place to sit or lie down. Let your mind focus on your breathing as you take a few deep breaths. Then choose whether to keep your eyes open or to close them. Start by gently tapping on the karate-chop point on the side of your hand.

### Round One

> *Side of hand: Even though I'm worried about not sleeping well, I love and accept myself.*
>
> *Side of hand: Even though I'm worried about not being able to sleep as I would like, I love and accept myself.*

*Side of the hand: Even though I'm worried about not sleeping well, I love and accept myself.*

*Eyebrow: I am worried about being able to sleep.*

*Side of eye: I am worried I won't sleep.*

*Under eye: Sometimes it takes a long time to get to sleep.*

*Under nose: I can lie there for hours trying to get to sleep.*

*Chin: I just want to get to sleep.*

*Collarbone: I want to be able to sleep well.*

*Underarm: I want to be able to stay asleep.*

*Top of head: I want to sleep well.*

## Round Two

*Eyebrow: What if I wake in the night?*

*Side of eye: What if I can't get back to sleep?*

*Under eye: I want to sleep through the night.*

*Under nose: I want to wake feeling refreshed.*

*Chin: I am worried about waking in the night.*

*Collarbone: I am worried about not sleeping.*

*Underarm: If I don't sleep well, it affects me.*

*Top of head: If I don't sleep well, it affects me.*

## Round Three

*Eyebrow: I help myself to feel calm.*

*Side of eye: I am helping myself to relax.*

*Under eye: I am choosing to help myself.*

*Under nose: I choose to look after myself.*

*Chin: I choose to be calmer.*

*Collarbone: I choose to be still.*

*Underarm: I choose to sleep.*

*Top of head: I choose to sleep.*

Gently stop tapping and allow yourself to be still. Take some deep breaths in and out. Feel into your body to assess it. Have you got any remaining tension left in your body? Is your mind still busy with thoughts? If you answer yes to either of these questions, it may be beneficial to continue to tap for some more rounds before reviewing these questions again. It is harder to get to sleep when we have tension in our bodies or when our minds are busy. With each round of tapping, you are sending signals that it is safe for you to go to sleep.

. . . . . . . . . . . . . . . . . . . . . .

If you are someone who often struggles with getting to sleep or sleeping through the night, it may help you to make a habit of doing this tapping practice every evening before bed for a few weeks. The more you practise tapping before bed the more your body will know what to expect. You will also become more familiar with the script and which phrases feel right for you. If you wake in the night, it is then easier to either tap in bed without having to read the script and to use phrases that feel helpful to you, or you can visualize tapping on the points. You may choose to repeat to yourself, 'It's safe to go back to sleep', whilst visualizing the tapping points or physically tapping on them. Keep repeating the same phrase while tapping. Hopefully, it will become easier and less stressful to try to get more sleep.

# Anxiety

We all have times when we feel anxious. It could be that we are feeling anxious about an upcoming event or conversation, or it may be that we are anxious about money, health or a loved one. It may be that you suffer from anxiety and you know you find it difficult to control. You may be anxious occasionally or it may be that you are anxious for periods of time. Tapping can help in all of these situations as it calms the nervous system and returns the body to a rest and digest state where everything can feel more manageable.

## TAPPING SCRIPT

Before you start to tap, rate your anxiety on a zero to 10 scale, with 10 being the most anxious you could be. Take a few deep breaths and maybe roll your shoulders back. You can use the script below, saying the words out loud or in your head. Start by tapping on the side of the hand and repeat this point three times.

### Round One

*Side of hand: Even though I'm feeling anxious, I deeply love and accept myself.*

*Side of hand: Even though I'm feeling anxious, I deeply love and accept myself.*

*Side of hand: Even though I'm feeling anxious, I deeply love and accept myself.*

*Eyebrow: Feeling anxious.*

*Side of eye: Feeling anxious.*

*Under eye: This anxiety.*

*Under nose: I can feel it in my body.*

*Chin: I can feel this anxiety in my body.*

Whilst tapping on your collarbone, think about where in your body you can feel that anxiety. Have you got a tightness in your stomach or a sickly feeling in your stomach? Maybe your shoulders feel really tense or you are clenching your jaw? Maybe you can feel it in your arms? It may be that your breath feels a bit tight. Think about where you feel that anxiety in your body. Focus on that part of your body now, as you tap.

*Underarm: I am thinking about where I feel that anxiety.*

*Top of head: Thinking about the area of my body where I am feeling anxious.*

## Round Two

*Eyebrow: This anxiety I can feel.*

*Side of eye: I can feel it in my body.*

*Under eye: I feel this anxiety in my body.*

*Under nose: I cannot seem to get rid of it.*

*Chin: I do not like how it is making me feel.*

*Collarbone: This anxiety in my body.*

*Underarm: I can feel this anxiety in my body.*

*Top of head: I feel this anxiety in my body.*

## Round Three

*Eyebrow: I breathe into my anxiety.*

*Side of eye: Breathing in and breathing out.*

*Under eye: Breathing in and breathing out.*

*Under nose: Breathing in and breathing out.*

*Chin: Breathing into this anxiety.*

*Collarbone: Noticing how those anxious thoughts feel now.*

*Underarm: Do I still feel the anxiety in the same place in my body?*

Take a moment to find where you feel anxiety in your body.

*Top of head: Noticing how I feel now.*

Gently stop tapping and take a deep breath in and out. Go back to that zero to 10 scale and think about how anxious you are feeling right now, with zero meaning you are not anxious at all, and 10 meaning you're the most anxious you can be. Hopefully, your number has gone down a little bit. You may need to carry on tapping for longer, or it may be that you feel that the scale is low enough if you are feeling calmer.

· · · · · · · · · · · · · · · · · · · · · ·

Practising tapping for anxiety regularly may make the script easier to remember. By feeling into your body and where you feel the anxiety in your body you become more aware. When you know where you tend to feel it, you might be able to recognize anxiety building and quickly tap to reduce it.

# When You Feel Vulnerable

We all have times in our lives when we feel vulnerable. It may be that we have had a diagnosis from the doctor that means we are at higher risk of a condition and we need to make lifestyle changes. It may be that we have been involved in a confrontation or a situation where we didn't feel safe. There can be many reasons why we might be feeling vulnerable. Some people see their own vulnerability as a sign of weakness, which they do not want others to notice; however, if they saw vulnerability in someone else they would not regard it as weakness. When we feel like this, it reflects a desire to hide how we are feeling from others. We may feel embarrassed that we are vulnerable or think that others will think less of us if we do not appear to be strong. I believe that we are being strong when we let our vulnerability show, that we are being brave, as it takes strength to admit we are feeling vulnerable.

## TAPPING SCRIPT

We can use tapping to acknowledge how we are feeling and to give ourselves a moment of quiet to breathe. Before you start tapping, rate on a zero to 10 scale how vulnerable you are feeling, with 10 being the most vulnerable and zero being the least. Take a few deep breaths before starting to tap on the side of the hand, and repeat this point three times.

### Round One

*Side of hand: Even though I am feeling vulnerable, I deeply love and accept myself.*

*Side of hand: Even though I am feeling vulnerable, I deeply love and accept myself.*

*Side of hand: Even though I am feeling vulnerable, I deeply love and accept myself.*

*Eyebrow: I am feeling vulnerable.*

*Side of eye: I am feeling vulnerable.*

*Under eye: I don't like feeling this way.*

*Under nose: I don't want others to see me this way.*

*Chin: I am feeling vulnerable.*

*Collarbone: I cannot help how I am feeling.*

*Underarm: I don't like feeling this way.*

*Top of head: I am feeling vulnerable.*

## Round Two

*Eyebrow: I do not feel strong.*

*Side of eye: I don't feel strong when I'm vulnerable.*

*Under eye: It feels like a weakness.*

*Under nose: It feels like I should hide it.*

*Chin: What would others think?*

*Collarbone: What would others think if they knew I was vulnerable?*

*Underarm: I don't see it as a weakness in others.*

*Top of head: So why would they see it as a weakness in me?*

## Round Three

*Eyebrow: I choose to acknowledge how I am feeling.*

*Side of eye: It is okay to be vulnerable.*

*Under eye: I can accept how I am feeling.*

*Under nose: It is okay to be vulnerable.*

*Chin: I choose to take deep breaths.*

*Collarbone: I breathe in deeply.*

*Underarm: I take a long breath out.*

*Top of head: It is okay to be vulnerable.*

When you stop tapping, give yourself a few minutes to continue taking some deeper breaths in and out. You may need to repeat this tapping script a few times to feel calmer and to help you accept how you are feeling at this time. Go back to the zero to 10 scale and consider how vulnerable you are feeling, with 10 being the most vulnerable.

. . . . . . . . . . . . . . . . . . . . . . .

We all feel vulnerable sometimes, and it is not something to be embarrassed about. By sharing that something is making you feel this way you take the power out of the vulnerability. You show strength when you show you are vulnerable. It is sometimes easier for others to communicate with you if they know what you are going through and how you are feeling. If we seem to go through life with nothing fazing us or bothering us it can make it harder for others to connect with us.

# Panic Attacks

Unfortunately, I know that there are quite few educators who experience panic attacks, either due to work or personal circumstances. I have spoken to people who have felt embarrassed by their panic attacks; they feel they should be able to control the attacks. Having a panic attack is nothing to be embarrassed or ashamed about. It is your body giving a very clear warning signal that it doesn't feel safe – it has gone into fight-or-flight mode. You are unable to think clearly during this time and it is hard to function well because your mind and body do not feel safe.

During a panic attack, your body is taken over by the hormones adrenaline and cortisol. These hormones cause the fight-or-flight reactions that may make you feel nauseous, make your heart beat much faster and cause you to breathe so fast that you hyperventilate. You can feel detached from your body and completely out of control.

Once you have experienced a panic attack, you are likely to worry about having another one and what that might look like or where you might be when it happens. I've known of teachers who appear to be keeping it together who then go home and have panic attacks. If you experience panic attacks, then tapping might be a tool that you would like to try. It is a gentle way to calm your nervous system whilst acknowledging what you are feeling at a point in time.

## TAPPING SCRIPT

This tapping script is to help you if you are experiencing a panic attack or if you are aware of your body's early warning signs that you are about to have a panic attack. Panic attacks are frightening and all-consuming. Your body and mind do not feel safe, so you experience a range of different thoughts and sensations that can be hard to get under control. By using the tapping script and saying the statements, you will send calming signals to your brain that will help raise serotonin levels and reduce cortisol levels, making you feel more in control.

Before you start tapping, rate your level of anxiety or feelings of panic on a zero to 10 scale, with 10 being the most anxious and panicked you could be and zero meaning that you are completely fine and that nothing is bothering you. Once you have your scaled number, make sure your feet are planted firmly on the floor and take three deep breaths in and out.

## Round One

*Side of hand: Even though I am having a panic attack, I am safe.*

*Side of hand: Even though I am having a panic attack and I do not know when it will stop, I am safe.*

*Side of hand: Even though I am having a panic attack, I am safe.*

*Eyebrow: Having a panic attack.*

*Side of eye: I do not feel safe.*

*Under eye: Having a panic attack.*

*Under nose: I do not feel safe.*

*Chin: Having a panic attack.*

*Collarbone: I do not feel safe.*

*Underarm: I want this to stop.*

*Top of head: I want this to stop.*

## Round Two

*Eyebrow: I do not like feeling like this.*

*Side of eye: I do not like feeling like this.*

*Under eye: My heart is racing.*

*Under nose: My breathing is fast.*

*Chin: My stomach is clenching.*

*Collarbone: I do not feel safe at the moment.*

*Underarm: I am having a panic attack.*

*Top of head: I am having a panic attack.*

## Round Three

*Eyebrow: I do not like feeling like this.*

*Side of eye: I want this to stop.*

*Under eye: I do not like feeling like this.*

*Under nose: I want this to stop.*

*Chin: I am aware how my body feels.*

*Collarbone: I am aware how my body feels.*

*Underarm: Breathing calm into my body.*

*Top of head: Breathing calm into my body.*

Pause your tapping for a moment and notice how you are feeling now on the zero to 10 scale, with 10 meaning you are still in a full panic attack and zero meaning you are completely calm. Hopefully, you will find your number has gone down slightly. You are aiming to try to get your score as low as possible, ideally under three. If your new number is over three, repeat the tapping practice until you feel calmer, and your score is lower. There is no specific number of sets of tapping rounds you should do. Sometimes you may find you feel calmer after one sequence of tapping rounds, at other times you may need to tap for much longer, depending on how you are feeling at the time.

. . . . . . . . . . . . . . . . . . . . . . .

If you have tried tapping and you are still experiencing a panic attack, please ask others for help. Talk to people you trust and share with them what you are experiencing. Talking to others can help.

# CHAPTER 9

# Tapping for Teaching

*'You can't stop the waves, but*
*you can learn to surf.'*

JON KABAT-ZINN

This chapter explores some of the unique challenges of teaching and how you can use tapping as a support. Teaching can feel like the sea, in that more tasks and jobs will always replace what you have just completed, there are always more things you could do. There will be times when it feels like everything is building up and mounting; you cannot stop things from happening, but you can begin to navigate and feel more in control. As it says in the quote above: 'You can't stop the waves, but you can learn to surf.' Consider the tapping scripts in the following pages as your surfboard. They are for teacher-specific situations that can be stress inducing: lesson observations, dealing with a difficult parent, having a bad day, end-of-term tiredness and coping with feelings following a safeguarding concern. This section is designed for you to dip into when needed and return to as many times as you wish. Each of the situations in this chapter can raise anxiety or worry levels, so you may find it useful to do several rounds of the tapping script you are using.

# A Bad Day

We have all experienced a bad day at work. A day that you can't wait to end because you are not sure how much longer you can keep it all together and remain sane! Those days can be caused by several reasons when you are teaching. It may be that you didn't sleep well the night before, so you are tired before you start the day. The school may be very short-staffed due to illness, which puts extra pressure on everyone else, so you feel more on edge. You could be dealing with very challenging behaviour in your class and no matter what strategies you try, and no matter how consistent you are, nothing seems to be making a difference. Over time, these pressures can be draining and wear you down, and in turn, this influences your perspective on the whole day. It could become a bad day because the photocopier is broken again and you cannot print all the resources that you spent hours preparing, and you need to completely re-think all your lessons for that day. Sometimes several of these things happen together and you feel like you can't catch a break. Sometimes we can deal with these situations, and we can cope, but at other times these things feel unmanageable, they can accumulate and overwhelm us.

You may have things going on at home too, which you cannot leave at the door when you enter school and remain on your mind throughout the day. Teaching can be an all-consuming profession. When your home life has challenges or is busy it can feel hard to stay on top of everything at work, which can then impact on the teaching experience too. In teaching, we are constantly looking after other people and considering their needs. At home, when a family member is ill then they will be on our minds. We often don't consider our own needs. When we are having a bad day, it may be because we have neglected our own needs for too long. If you find you are having a series of bad days, it may be worth looking at your self-care to make sure you are thinking about your needs *(see page 55)*.

Sometimes just recognizing that you are having a bad day can make a big difference. Acknowledging how you are feeling and noticing what made the day seem bad can help. Often this negative factor was only one small part of your whole day, but it plays on your mind and is hard to avoid. Tapping can help you to move past the belief that everything is going wrong and focus on other parts of the day that hopefully went well. Our negative bias can make us focus more on the negative parts of the day than the positive.

## TAPPING SCRIPT

Before you start tapping, place your feet evenly on the ground and take a few deep breaths. Think about your day and how it is making you feel. Then rate how you are feeling about your day on a zero to 10 scale, with 10 being the worst day you could possibly have.

### Round One

> *Side of hand: Even though I have had a bad day, and I'm feeling awful, I love and accept myself.*
>
> *Side of hand: Even though I have had a bad day, and I'm questioning what I'm doing, I love and accept myself.*
>
> *Side of hand: Even though I have had a bad day, and I'm feeling awful, I love and accept myself.*
>
> *Eyebrow: I've had a bad day.*

*Side of eye: Everything seems to be going wrong.*

*Under eye: I've had a bad day.*

*Under nose: I'm questioning myself about what happened.*

*Chin: I'm blaming myself and others.*

*Collarbone: I'm feeling angry and upset.*

*Underarm: I've had a bad day.*

*Top of head: My negative thoughts are taking over.*

## Round Two

*Eyebrow: I've had a bad day.*

*Side of eye: It's making me feel* (insert how you're feeling).

*Under eye: I don't like feeling like this.*

*Under nose: I don't feel like I've done my best teaching.*

*Chin: I don't feel good about myself.*

*Collarbone: I don't feel good about myself.*

*Underarm: I don't want to feel like this.*

*Top of head: I don't want to feel like this.*

## Round Three

*Eyebrow: I'm having a bad day.*

*Side of eye: Everyone has bad days.*

*Under eye: I'm having a bad day.*

*Under nose: Everyone has bad days.*

*Chin: I choose for my day to improve.*

*Collarbone: I choose to feel better.*

*Underarm: I choose for my day to improve.*

*Top of head: I choose to feel better.*

Gently stop tapping and take a few deep breaths. Think about how you are feeling now after tapping and rate on a zero to 10 scale how you feel, with 10 meaning that you still feel awful and zero that you feel fine. Hopefully, your number has gone down, and you feel a bit calmer about your day. You may find that you need to do a few sets of tapping rounds depending on how bad your day has been. Do as many rounds as you need to until you feel your scaled rating go down.

. . . . . . . . . . . . . . . . . . . . . . .

If possible, see if you can think about one or two positives about your day; these can be small things such as someone smiling or saying good morning. Taking time to notice a few small positive things can help shift your feelings about the day because it alleviates some of the negative bias.

Depending on the reason for your bad day, it may be useful to speak to a colleague, family member or friend about your day too.

## Monitoring

When we have our lessons observed or have staff, senior leaders or inspectors drop in to our classrooms to see our practice, it can create a nervous energy. However positively the lesson observations or drop-in sessions are done, as teachers we feel judged and that we need to prove that we are good at our jobs. We feel on edge and nervous as we know that it is unlikely that our lessons will go completely to plan. We have fears that something will go wrong with the technology that we plan to use. If this happens, we may feel the panic rise within us as we try to resolve the technology problem quickly, whilst also holding the class together and monitoring everything the pupils are doing. Alternatively, we abandon the resources we had carefully selected and prepared for the lesson and try to sustain momentum in our teaching.

We worry about the behaviour of pupils in our class, especially if we have children with particularly challenging behaviour or complex needs. We don't ever know how these children are going to react, especially if they are really struggling at the time of the observation. We question how the observer may judge our responses to these situations. We know these struggles can impact the pace of learning in the lesson and we may worry about how they may reflect on us, as teachers.

When these negative worries bombard us our anxiety about having lessons observed is heightened. If we know our lesson is going to be observed, we often spend much longer planning it as we want it to reflect the best of our practice. Sometimes we can put too much pressure on ourselves to try to get everything just so. When this happens, we can become more agitated. Our class can sense when we are not our usual selves, and this can have an impact on the behaviour in the lesson. Tapping can make us feel calmer at this time, which can help us to present the best version of ourselves.

We can tap on our worries about what could go wrong, on the self-doubts about our planning, teaching and resources. We can also tap after we have been observed if we find that we are being over-critical about our teaching. Tapping will help us to acknowledge all of the fears that we have and help us to move forward with more clarity in the way we wish.

# TAPPING SCRIPT

Before you start to tap, place your feet evenly on the ground and take a few deep breaths. Take a moment to consider what it is about the lesson observation that you are worried about most – maybe the fear of doing something wrong, the feeling of being judged or not being good enough, the worry about class behaviour or feeling so anxious you can't talk properly. Whatever your biggest fear is, give it a rating on a zero to 10 scale, with 10 being the most worried you could be and zero being that you have no fear.

Start tapping on the side of the hand and repeat the phrases below either in your head or out loud.

## Round One

> *Side of hand: Even though I have this lesson observation and I feel really nervous, I accept myself and the feelings I am experiencing.*

> *Side of hand: Even though I have this lesson observation and I am overthinking it, I accept myself and the feelings I am experiencing.*

> *Side of hand: Even though I have this lesson observation and I feel really nervous, I accept myself and the feelings I am experiencing.*

> *Eyebrow: I have this lesson observation.*

> *Side of eye: I'm feeling really nervous.*

> *Under eye: What if it goes wrong?*

> *Under nose: What will they think about me?*

> *Chin: What will they say about me?*

> *Collarbone: I feel like I'm going to be judged.*

Underarm: *I feel like I'm going to be judged.*

Top of head: *I'm worried about my lesson observation.*

## Round Two

Eyebrow: *I'm feeling worried.*

Side of eye: *What if something goes wrong?*

Under eye: *What if something goes wrong?*

Under nose: *What will I do?*

Chin: *How will the class react?*

Collarbone: *What will the observers think of me?*

Underarm: *What will they think of me?*

Top of head: *What if they think I'm not a good teacher?*

## Round Three

Eyebrow: *I feel like I'm going to be judged.*

Side of eye: *I feel like I'm going to be judged.*

Under eye: *I'm questioning what I've planned.*

Under nose: *I'm overthinking things I do every day.*

Chin: *I know how to do my job.*

Collarbone: *I know how to do my job.*

Underarm: *I can do my job well.*

Top of head: *I can do my job well.*

When you stop tapping take a few deep breaths. Think about how you are feeling now on a zero to 10 scale, with 10 meaning you are the most anxious you can be. Hopefully, your number rating has reduced, and you are feeling a bit calmer and in control.

. . . . . . . . . . . . . . . . . . . . . . .

A certain amount of stress about lesson observations is very usual and can help you. When you have some adrenaline in your body, you may be at your peak performance. Too much can make you feel out of control, so tapping reduces feelings of stress and you can teach in your best way.

Before you get any feedback from the lesson, reflect on how you feel the lesson went – try not to be critical but find the positives in it. You probably won't get direct feedback from external inspectors. If you get feedback from your observer, try to listen to everything they have to say without only listening to the areas for improvement. It is easy for our brain's negative bias to take over and for us not to hear the positives, so I encourage you to listen carefully for what went well.

## Awkward Conversations with Parents

It doesn't matter how good you are at your job, or how much time and consideration you may have put into something, you can still end up with a parental complaint. When a complaint is made it can make you feel judged and question what you have been doing. How the school deals with the situation can make a big difference to how you feel about it.

Due to the nature of social media, small parental niggles shared in online groups can quickly become blown out of proportion. Often teachers don't know about the rumbling conversations on social media until they come to a crescendo. At this point, we may be dealing with very agitated parents who have been spurred on by other parents. As teachers, we may find ourselves going into conversations where we don't know the full extent of a parent's concern or worry.

Concerns or complaints may arrive by email or through the school office and they can feel like a bombardment of information. I think it is important to choose when to read or listen to this information. It will not be good for you or your class to receive the information when you are just about to teach or are in the middle of teaching a lesson. We can't help but react to these kinds of correspondence instantly. When we are not teaching, we can give ourselves more time to process the information and we have the opportunity to discuss it with colleagues and get their advice.

I find the best way to respond to a concern is to speak to a parent either face to face or on the phone, so that you have a two-way conversation where the parent can feel fully heard and you have the opportunity to listen and respond appropriately. I often start these conversations with 'I'm sorry you are feeling worried', or 'I have received your message and wanted to have the opportunity to discuss this with you further.' When you speak to parents in person rather than via email, they can hear in your voice that you want to help them. Emails can be misinterpreted, depending on the tone in which they are read.

Although we can be triggered by these messages or criticisms, as they feel like a personal attack, most of the time parents are genuinely concerned. They have heard one side of a situation from their child and, understandably, they just want the best for their child. They may also bring their own school experiences to the situation.

I find it is always helpful to discuss a complaint with a colleague. Share how you are feeling, your viewpoint of the situation and possible points that may be useful to raise with the parent during the discussion.

Even though we feel heightened emotions, it is important for us to remain professional and calm during the conversation, which can be difficult. I find that tapping before going into these situations helps me to feel more level and composed. Tapping allows us to acknowledge how we are feeling at the time, whilst calming our nervous system and making it easier for us to communicate in the way we wish. If you need to wait until the day after a concern has been raised to speak to the parent, then it helps to tap the night before and on the morning of the conversation.

## TAPPING SCRIPT

Sit or stand with your feet placed firmly on the ground. Start by taking a few deep breaths in and out. Think about how you are feeling at this time and rate it on a zero to 10 scale, with 10 meaning you feel the most triggered and zero meaning the least. Once you have your scaled score, start tapping on the karate-chop point on the side of your hand.

### Round One

*Side of hand: Even though I have to speak to this parent, I accept myself and know I am doing the best I can.*

*Side of hand: Even though I have to deal with this parental complaint, and it makes me feel angry, I accept my feelings and know I am doing the best I can.*

*Side of hand: Even though I have to deal with this situation, and it makes me feel angry, I accept my feelings and know I am doing the best I can.*

*Eyebrow: I've had a complaint from a parent.*

*Side of eye: It makes me feel cross.*

*Under eye: I am doing the best that I can.*

*Under nose: But my best is being criticized.*

*Chin: I feel like I am being judged.*

*Collarbone: I'm doing the best I can.*

*Underarm: But my best is being criticized.*

*Top of head: I feel like I am being judged and my professionalism is being criticized.*

## Round Two

*Eyebrow: I don't want to talk to this parent.*

*Side of eye: I wish they would leave me alone.*

*Under eye: I'm working so hard.*

*Under nose: But still, I'm receiving complaints.*

*Chin: I'm working so hard.*

*Collarbone: Trying to do the best for the children I teach.*

*Underarm: I wish they would leave me alone.*

*Top of head: I don't want to talk to them.*

## Round Three

*Eyebrow: I need to let them feel heard.*

*Side of eye: I need to hear their side of the story.*

*Under eye: They just want what's best for their child.*

*Under nose: They don't understand that I want the best for their child.*

*Chin: We both want what is best for the child.*

*Collarbone: We both want what is best for the child.*

*Underarm: I can be compassionate when I talk to them.*

*Top of head: I can protect myself and still be compassionate.*

## Round Four

*Eyebrow: I am professional.*

*Side of eye: I can stay calm when I speak.*

*Under eye: I can listen to what they want to say.*

*Under nose: I am not being attacked.*

*Chin: They just want to know their child is safe and happy.*

*Collarbone: They are sharing their worries.*

*Underarm: I am professional.*

*Top of head: I can stay calm when I speak to them.*

When you have completed your rounds of tapping, take a few deep breaths in and out. Think about how triggered you are feeling now and rate it on a zero to 10 scale, with 10 meaning you are still highly triggered. Hopefully, your rating has gone down, meaning that you will be able to have a calmer conversation with the parents. If your rating is still high, try taking some more deep breaths and tap again.

. . . . . . . . . . . . . . . . . . . . . . . . .

Once you have had the conversation with the parents, I recommend that you speak to a colleague to share how it went and how you are feeling. It can help you to talk it through and it helps your colleagues understand what you are dealing with. Also, sharing these conversations with members of the senior leadership team can help them support you.

## End-of-Term Tiredness

Inevitably, tiredness takes hold towards the end of every term, when it becomes difficult to get out of bed in the morning, as you often wake still feeling tired. You may feel tiredness in your whole body. In the evening, you may find it harder to focus as your body sends signals to slow down; it's running out of energy. You may find that any illness you have lingers longer than normal at this time. Unfortunately, the period nearing the end of term coincides with many of the bigger events in the teaching year, such as productions or performances that require creativity, stamina and enthusiasm. Other busy occasions include Christmas, welcoming a new cohort, sports day and supporting leavers in their transition to the next stage. All these important times in the school year create opportunities to celebrate as a whole-school community. They are when everyone comes together to celebrate enriched learning opportunities and to recognize individual and group talent and achievements.

Often, these events happen at times when teachers are feeling run down or tired; however, as professionals we keep going, knowing what a difference these opportunities make to the school community.

Although we know that a holiday and chance to recuperate is coming soon, we don't necessarily consider the long-term impact on our health when we ignore warning signals from our bodies – which can be screaming out to slow down and rest. When we get very tired, we may experience many physical, mental and emotional symptoms. We may find that we feel overwhelmed with tasks that at other times we take in our stride. We may find that we have new or returning aches and pains as our bodies try different ways to encourage us to slow down. We may get upset easily and take offence about something someone has said that we would usually put into context and not give another thought.

In schools many staff reach a wave of tiredness at a similar time, so there may be many people in the staff team all trying their best when they are shattered. This doesn't make for the best working environment for adults or learning environment for children. The sugar-laden treats that appear in the staffroom are quickly consumed as teachers try to get extra energy into their bodies.

When the end-of-term tiredness hits, there are some things that you can do to look after yourself. Firstly, treat yourself to some early nights, as sleep is going to be the best remedy. Try using a meal planner so you don't need to think about what you are going to eat each day, and your food shop becomes easier. Meal planning can also help you to make sure you have healthy, balanced meals that will look after your nutritional needs. Plan something relaxing and enjoyable for the weekends so you have something to look forward to, but that will not require too much energy. Be kind to yourself at work – can you leave slightly earlier than usual at the end of the day? Can you make sure you stop at lunchtime to talk to other adults and eat a proper meal? Your body will thank you for taking a break.

# TAPPING SCRIPT

Tapping when you are tired helps you to feel more energized and can be a simple way to tune into your body and how you are feeling. Start by taking a few deep breaths with your feet flat on the floor. Rate on a zero to 10 scale your current level of tiredness with 10 being the most tired you could feel.

## Round One

*Side of hand: Even though I feel completely exhausted, I choose to pause and look after myself now.*

*Side of hand: Even though I feel completely exhausted, and I need to keep working, I choose to pause and look after myself now.*

*Side of hand: Even though I feel completely exhausted, I choose to pause and look after myself now.*

*Eyebrow: Feeling completely exhausted.*

*Side of eye: I'm finding it hard to get up in the mornings.*

*Under eye: I still feel tired when I wake up.*

*Under nose: Everyone seems to be tired.*

*Chin: Just need to get to the end of term.*

*Collarbone: I recognize that I'm feeling tired.*

*Underarm: I acknowledge that I'm feeling tired.*

*Top of head: I acknowledge that I'm feeling tired.*

## Round Two

*Eyebrow: I acknowledge that I'm feeling tired.*

*Side of eye: I choose to slow down.*

*Under eye: I acknowledge that I'm feeling tired.*

*Under nose: I choose to look after myself.*

*Chin: I acknowledge that I'm feeling tired.*

*Collarbone: I choose to slow down.*

*Underarm: I acknowledge that I'm feeling tired.*

*Top of head: I choose to look after myself.*

## Round Three

*Eyebrow: I acknowledge how I am feeling.*

*Side of eye: I choose to look after myself.*

*Under eye: I acknowledge how I am feeling.*

*Under nose: I choose to breathe deeply into my body.*

*Chin: I choose to breathe energy into my body.*

*Collarbone: I choose to breathe deeply into my body.*

*Underarm: I choose to breathe energy into my body.*

*Top of head: I choose to breathe energy into my body.*

When you have finished the rounds of tapping take a few deep breaths. Rate how tired you feel on a zero to 10 scale with 10 being exhausted. This tapping sequence is different to others you may have tried in this book as it helps to energize you when you are tired. First, we acknowledged how we were feeling and then we tapped on how we chose to feel. It may be useful to do this tapping sequence a few times to help you feel more energized.

. . . . . . . . . . . . . . . . . . . . . . . .

When it comes to the end of term and all staff and children are feeling tired it can sometimes be hard to keep the environment feeling calm and a safe space to learn. By practising tapping, you are lowering your cortisol levels, so you feel calmer in yourself. This tapping script can help you feel more energized and able to cope with your day. That may then have a ripple effect through the school – if you feel calm and energized it will help others to feel the same.

## Concerns About a Child

In teaching, there are often child protection safeguarding issues or pupils who cause you concern. I think this is the hardest part of our job – suspecting or knowing that a child is in a vulnerable or damaging situation and feeling powerless to help them. We need to recognize changes in a child's behaviour and pass on any concerns to safeguarding leads at school – while knowing that all we can do is be there for the child if they want to talk.

In these situations, although we feel powerless, our small acts of kindness can make a big difference to the day-to-day life of a vulnerable child. It really helps a child to know that they have a safe adult to talk to and who understands that they are having a difficult time. Small acts of kindness may include giving that child more attention in class or checking in with them more often. You may give them a thumbs up or smile to check in – nonverbal checks can be very supportive. You can ask the child if there is anything that would help them at this time. All these actions help the child to feel they are not alone.

Any child protection or safeguarding scenario plays on a teacher's mind long after leaving the school building for the night. It tends to be something that haunts you and is hard to get out of your mind. I know that on these days I go home and give my own children and husband an extra-long hug. I feel lucky about my own situation and feel sad about the difficulties facing the children I'm teaching. There is a feeling of frustration that there should be more that I could do and a certain amount of anger that any child should be in a vulnerable position.

Sometimes we don't have any evidence, but we have a gut instinct that something isn't right – maybe you've noticed a change in behaviour or a child is being more emotional, and you sense something might be wrong. We may have a worrying feeling, knowing that something doesn't feel right for a child. When you have these gut instinct feelings, it is important to share them with your designated safeguard leads – even if you don't have evidence – as others may have noticed things too. Every separate thing may together build a picture of what is going on for that child. Sometimes your safeguard lead may know something about the family that makes sense of the child's change in behaviour.

We can use tapping to help us reduce these haunting feelings and as a coping mechanism when we are holding worries and concerns for children and adults whom we support. When we are holding these big worries or concerns then we often have tension in our bodies. Tension is a good thing to tap on as it helps us to get out of our head thinking and repetitive thoughts, and focus on our body.

# TAPPING SCRIPT

Before we start tapping, take a moment to sit in a comfortable position with your feet placed on the floor. Take a few deep breaths and see if you are holding tension anywhere in your body. Then rate your current level of worry on a zero to 10 scale, with 10 being the most worried and concerned you could be feeling and zero meaning you have no worries. When you have your number, start tapping on the side of your hand.

## Round One

*Side of hand: Even though I am concerned about this child, I allow myself to relax.*

*Side of hand: Even though I am concerned about this child and I can't stop thinking about them, I allow myself to relax.*

*Side of hand: Even though I am concerned about this child, I allow myself to relax.*

*Eyebrow: All these worries.*

*Side of eye: I have so many concerns.*

*Under eye: I can't stop thinking about them.*

*Under nose: What are they going through?*

*Chin: What are they coping with?*

*Collarbone: They shouldn't have to deal with this.*

*Underarm: I feel powerless.*

*Top of head: I want to do more to help them.*

## Round Two

*Eyebrow: Worried about this child.*

*Side of eye: Feeling powerless.*

*Under eye: I'm struggling to stop thinking about this.*

*Under nose: My mind keeps coming back to these thoughts.*

*Chin: I feel this tension in my body.*

*Collarbone: I feel this tension in my* (fill in where you feel the tension; it may be your jaw, shoulders, stomach, chest or somewhere else).

*Underarm: I feel this tension in my body.*

*Top of head: This tension that is hard to release.*

## Round Three

*Eyebrow: I know there is nothing I can do right now.*

*Side of eye: I am creating a safe school environment.*

*Under eye: I listen when they talk.*

*Under nose: I hold a safe space.*

*Chin: I watch for changes in behaviour.*

*Collarbone: I am doing what I can right now.*

*Underarm: I'm ready to release some of the tension.*

*Top of head: I'm ready to release some of the tension.*

Pause tapping and rate the level of worry and tension in your body on the zero to 10 scale, with 10 being the most worried and highest level of tension you could have in your body and zero meaning that there isn't any tension or worry in your body. Once you have your number, decide if you are feeling better or whether you would benefit from repeating the tapping meditation either now or in the future. You are aiming to get your number as low as feels right for you.

. . . . . . . . . . . . . . . . . . . . . . . .

Safeguarding concerns are always going to leave us with worries because we want to protect the children in our school. I think there is some reassurance in knowing that we are doing everything we can at the time and that we will continue to be an advocate for the child. I think it helps the child to know that school is a safe space and that there are always adults there whom they can trust and who care for them.

You can use tapping to help you with many worries or concerns. You can use your own words as you tap to acknowledge how you are feeling at the time. If you are unsure of the words to use, simply tap on each of the tapping points and breathe in and out as you tap, without saying anything.

# Conclusion

*'What you pay attention to grows. Pay attention to
your loveliness, your magnificent self. Begin now.'*

GENEEN ROTH

When one person is feeling positive, capable and motivated,
it has a ripple effect on those around them, enabling their
family, colleagues and students to feel the impact. As teachers, we
can motivate and nurture each other to continue self-care practices
so they become part of everyday life.

## Being Part of a Community

When you work in a school you become part of its community.
You become an important link that helps the school to run
smoothly and helps children to thrive. Being part of the school
community is a two-way process: You need to feel nurtured by
the community and the community needs your support and ideas.
To work effectively in a school environment, you need to allow
your personality to shine through. When school leaders interview
people to join the staff, they are looking for who will fit in with the
existing team, whilst being authentically themselves.

To be yourself in a school, you do not need to share everything about yourself, but it is okay to show vulnerability. When you are having a hard time, share it with someone you trust at work. There are times at school when you need to leave what is happening in your life outside school and there will be other times when this is not possible. At times like this, speak to a member of your leadership team to get support. All schools should have people you can speak to if you need help. Many schools buy into counselling and support services that can often be accessed remotely. Schools invest in this when they can, as they know the pressures teachers are under and how important it is to get support. If you are really struggling with your wellbeing, please speak to a member of the leadership team, someone in school you trust or your doctor.

There are times when you are teaching when it can feel like an act – you need to show your enthusiasm and positivity when you teach even when that might not be how you are feeling. You must show up as your best self on any given day as that is what the pupils deserve. Some days your best self will not be the same as others; we are all human so some days may feel harder than others. Some days your best self will be 50 per cent of what you can give on other days and that is okay; we cannot all be working at our optimum all the time. That is why we are part of a team – we support and nurture each other, and when one person is having a hard time, the team can help.

There will be times when you go into the staffroom and celebrate an individual personal achievement or a great lesson; there will also be times when you share things that had not gone as planned. At other times you may need to go into the staffroom just to sit quietly while everything goes on around you. All of these ways of being are okay and completely normal. Try not to always talk about what has gone wrong unless you need to vent. Try to join in with what has been funny or humorous as this will help to lighten your mood. When everyone is being negative it can lower the energy in the room. If the conversation can be more balanced, then everyone can get support when they need it and celebrate when possible.

Every individual on the staff team will have their own strengths and talents. By celebrating our uniqueness, we can help to create teams that build on everyone's passions and talents. This can only happen if staff are open and honest about themselves and share what enthuses them. We can inspire others with our strengths and support them; in turn they are likely to do the same for us, creating a strong community where everyone feels valued and supported.

# A Final Word

My aim in writing this book was to provide teachers with a practical guide to help reduce stress and prioritize self-care. I know teaching is hard work, but I also know it is an amazing job. We have the opportunity as teachers to enhance pupils' lives. We can only do that effectively if we look after ourselves and our own needs. We must prioritize our self-care to help us feel calmer and make the best decisions for ourselves and those we support. I sincerely hope that you have found strategies and ideas in this book that help you to look after yourself so that you can continue to do an incredible job and be happy in your life. Teaching can be all-consuming if we let it be. We have the choice to create more happiness in our lives by making small changes. All those small changes that support our self-care make a big difference to how we feel each day.

## THINGS TO PONDER

- What are your next steps in self-care?

- How are you going to create a self-care routine that supports you?

- Who will you go to for support when you need it?

- What are you grateful for right now?

- Which ideas and strategies are you going to keep practising?

To answer this last question about which ideas and strategies in this book you are going to keep practising, you may like to flick back through the book to exercises or ideas that resonated with you. Mark these with a sticky note for easy reference when you need it.

Teaching is known for being one of the best and most worthwhile professions in the world, because every day we can make a positive difference to our students and those around us. We help to provide stability and a place of calm and safety. We are privileged to help nurture the grown-ups of the future. We get to be creative, challenged, inspired and passionate! Our days are varied and stimulating with two days never being the same. To do all this we need to find a balance between giving our all to do the best job we can and enjoying other aspects of our lives. I hope you have found strategies and ideas in this book to help you thrive and continue to love teaching. I wish you a happy life and teaching career!

# Resources

Below, you'll find details of wellbeing support organizations in your home country.

## Australia

**Beyond Blue** offers free confidential counselling and provides information to help all Australians experience good mental health.
*1300 22 4636*
*www.beyondblue.org.au*

**Head to Health** provides mental health information and support.
*1800 595 212*
*www.headtohealth.gov.au*

**Reach Out** lists wellbeing resources for teachers.
*schools.au.reachout.com*

## Canada

**Canadian Mental Health Association** gives help to anyone in crisis.
*9-8-8*
*cmha.ca*

**The Public Health Agency of Canada** lists mental health resources in every province and territory.
*www.canada.ca/en/public-health.html*

## Ireland

**The Irish National Teachers' Organisation (INTO)** is the country's oldest and largest trade union and offers advice and support on how to support your wellbeing.
*02890 381 455*
*www.into.ie*

## United Kingdom

**Education Support Partnership Charity** supports the wellbeing of school staff. Their website includes videos and articles on different areas of teacher wellbeing.
*08000 562 561*
*www.educationsupport.org.uk*

**Samaritans** is a charity that offers support to anyone in emotional distress, struggling to cope or at risk of suicide. It also operates in the Republic of Ireland.
*116 123*
*www.samaritans.org*

## United States of America

**Mental Health America** is a nonprofit dedicated to the promotion of mental health, wellbeing and illness prevention. It runs a crisis call centre and 'warmlines' across the country.
*988*
*mhanational.org*

**The Wellbeing Project** runs The Teacher Wellbeing Group, which supports the mental health of educators worldwide through pioneering research and global advocacy efforts.
*wellbeing-project.org*

# Endnotes

## Introduction

1. Cope, A. and Whittaker, A. (2012), *The Art of Being Brilliant*. Croydon: Capstone, pp.165–172.

2. PA Media (2022), '44% of teachers in England plan to quit within five years', *The Guardian*, 11 April 2022: https://www.theguardian.com/education/2022/apr/11/teachers-england-plan-to-quit-workloads-stress-trust [Accessed 11 February 2024].

3. CooperGibson Research (2018), 'Factors affecting teacher retention: qualitative investigation', Department for Education: https://assets.publishing.service.gov.uk/media/5aa15d24e5274a53c0b29341/Factors_affecting_teacher_retention_-_qualitative_investigation.pdf, pp.5–6 [Accessed 11 February 2024].

## Chapter 2: Everyday Teaching

1. Stibich, M. (2023), '10 Big Benefits of Smiling', verywellmind.com: https://www.verywellmind.com/top-reasons-to-smile-every-day-2223755 [Accessed 16 February 2024].

2. Dix, P. (2023), 'Positive Noticing Day', Positive Noticing: https://www.positivenoticingday.com/ [Accessed 17 February 2024].

## Chapter 4: Introduction to Mindfulness

1. Kabat-Zinn, J. (2020), 'Mindfulness-Based Stress Reduction', mbsrtraining.com: https://mbsrtraining.com/mindfulness-based-stress-reduction/ [Accessed 17 February 2024].

2. Williams, M. and Penman, D. (2011), *Mindfulness: A Practical Guide to Finding Peace in a Frantic World*. London: Piatkus.

3. Kabat-Zinn, J. *op.cit.*

4. Mautz, S. (2019), 'Harvard Study: 47 Percent of the Time You're Doing This 1 (Fixable) Thing That Kills Your Happiness', Inc.com: https://www.inc.com/scott-mautz/harvard-study-47-percent-of-time-youre-doing-this-1-fixable-thing-that-kills-your-happiness.html [Accessed 17 February 2024].

5. Kabat-Zinn, J. (2020), *Full Catastrophe Living: How to Cope with Stress, Pain and Illness Using Mindfulness Meditation*. London: Piatkus, pp.31–33.

## Chapter 5: Short Mindfulness Practices

1. Kabat Zinn, J. (2020), 'Body Scan Meditations', mbsrtraining.com: https://mbsrtraining.com/mindfulness-exercises-by-jon-kabat-zinn/body-scan-meditation/ [Accessed 18 February 2024].

## Chapter 6: Mindful Awareness

1. Antanaityte, N. (2023), 'Mind Matters: How to Effortlessly Have More Positive Thoughts', Mind Matters: TLEX Institute: https://tlexinstitute.com/how-to-effortlessly-have-more-positive-thoughts/ [Accessed 18 February 2024].

2. Ryff, C. (2022), 'Positive Psychology: Looking Back and Looking Forward', Frontiers in Psychology: https://www.frontiersin.org/articles/10.3389/fpsyg.2022.840062/full#Recent%20Work%20in%20Positive%20Psychology [Accessed 18 February 2024].

3. Morin, S. (2015), '7 Scientifically Proven Benefits of Gratitude', *Psychology Today*: https://www.psychologytoday.com/us/blog/what-mentally-strong-people-dont-do/201504/7-scientifically-proven-benefits-of-gratitude [Accessed 18 February 2024].

4. *Ibid.*

5. Emmons, R. (2003), 'Gratitude and Well-Being', *Gratitude Works*: https://emmons.faculty.ucdavis.edu/gratitude-and-well-being/ [Accessed 18 February 2024].

6. Weir, K. (2020), 'Nurtured by Nature', *American Psychological Association*, 51(3): https://www.apa.org/monitor/2020/04/nurtured-nature [Accessed 18 February 2024].

## Chapter 7: Introduction to Tapping

1. Feinstein, D., et al., (2005), *The Healing Power of EFT & Energy Psychology: Tap into your body's energy to change your life for the better.* US: Piatkus, pp.28–49.

2. Footman, J. (2018), 'NICE Recommendations for EFT', EFT International: https://eftinternational.org/nice-recommendations-for-eft/ [Accessed 18 February 2024].

3. Church, D. (2013), 'Clinical EFT as an Evidence-Based Practice for the Treatment of Psychological and Physiological Conditions', *Psychology*, 4, 645–654. doi: 10.4236/psych.2013.48092.

4. Hari, J. (2022), *Stolen Focus: Why You Can't Pay Attention.* London: Bloomsbury, pp.46–58.

# Acknowledgements

There is an African proverb that says it takes a village to raise a child; that it's not just the immediate family who help children fulfil their potential, but the community and extended family, as well as being in a safe and loving environment. I believe that it takes a tribe to help you to thrive! I'm fortunate to be surrounded by a wonderful tribe of people who nurture, challenge and believe in me – to you all, I thank you from the bottom of my heart.

I know that I have an amazing tribe of friends who will ask how things are going, give advice, stomp in the woods to talk things through and support me step by step through the easiest of technical procedures that I find challenging. I truly thank all of my friends (you know who you are), but a few special shoutouts: Claire, Sue and The Jordan Burrows for being super friends. Lisa for the tapping swaps. The Loopy Lemon-Lime Four Blondes and Their Big Fat Shoes, who are there for all the big and small moments in life. To the wonderful Wilsons, including friend 247 – you are friends that have become family. Dylan will forever be in our hearts and is so dearly missed.

A huge thanks to my Mum, who has always been my rock – you give the best advice, listen carefully and care deeply about us all. Together with Brian, you form the ultimate team. I thank you both for always listening to my next new idea and encouraging me to pursue my dreams and creativity. Thanks to Paul, Karan, Chloe, Wendy, Tim and Mae for your encouragement. I feel lots of gratitude also for our whole extended family – thank you for your love and support.

A massive thank you to Team St Lawrence! What an amazing school and community to be part of. So many of the St Lawrence team have helped with different aspects of creating this book: from early chapter proofreading to title suggestions, support with social media to taking photos for my website and book. Thanks to Karen for designing my logo. Thanks to Sue and Gill for always listening. A bigshout out to Gordon and Geoff for taking photos. A heartfelt thanks to Kerry, my Headteacher, who has supported me, coached me and believed in this book from the start. I feel honoured and grateful to be part of Team St Lawrence – it truly is a special school to work in.

I feel extremely grateful that Hay House saw something in my book and decided to publish it. I don't think I'll ever forget the moment that Michelle Pilley told me that I had won a publishing contract. It has been a privilege and pleasure to work with the talented Hay House team, but special thanks need to go to Rebecca who has been so kind, nurturing and professional in guiding me through the publishing process and answering my many questions. I also owe a huge thanks to Louise for your sensitive and thorough editing, and to Tom for raising my understanding of marketing and for being so approachable. Thank you to everyone at Hay House who has helped get this book into the world and welcomed me into the Hay House family.

A massive thank you to Abi and Jacob for making it great to be a Mum. Dad and I are so proud of you both – the amazing adults you are becoming and how you are following your dreams. Our hope for you both is that you always feel loved and are happy, in whatever you choose to do. We love you both with all our hearts.

Finally, the biggest amount of gratitude goes to Simon, my lobster and biggest cheerleader. You have always believed in me and supported me. Thank you for sharing your life with me – I love you more than words.

Geoff Lawrence

# About the Author

**Michelle Auton** has been a primary school teacher for over 25 years and an Assistant Headteacher for over a decade. In that time, she has worked hard to create a nurturing and safe environment in her schools for both children and staff to thrive.

In 2015, she learned how mindfulness and tapping could support her to be a great teacher, mum and wife whilst maintaining balance in her life. After recognizing the benefits, she trained to be an EFT Tapping practitioner and Mindfulness-Based Stress Reduction teacher and has since delivered many courses on these topics. She has brought this work into local schools to support teachers and now shares them in this, her first book.

michelleauton.com

@michelleauton

@michelleauton2

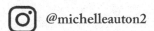

@michelleauton5956

## About the Author

# MEDITATE.
# VISUALIZE.
# LEARN.

*Get the* **Empower You**
Unlimited Audio *Mobile App*

## Get unlimited access to the entire Hay House audio library!

**You'll get:**

- 500+ inspiring and life-changing **audiobooks**
- 700+ ad-free **guided meditations** for sleep, healing, relaxation, spiritual connection, and more
- Hundreds of audios **under 20 minutes** to easily fit into your day
- **Exclusive content** *only* for subscribers
- **New audios** added every week
- No credits, **no limits**

Listen to the audio version of this book for **FREE!**

 ★★★★★ **I ADORE this app.** I use it almost every day. Such a blessing. – Aya Lucy Rose "

Scan me with your phone camera!

**TRY FOR FREE!**
Go to: hayhouse.com/listen-free

HAY HOUSE

CONNECT WITH

# HAY HOUSE
## ONLINE

🌐 hayhouse.co.uk    **f** @hayhouse

📷 @hayhouseuk    𝕏 @hayhouseuk

▶ @hayhouseuk    ♪ @hayhouseuk

*Find out all about our latest books & card decks • Be the first
to know about exclusive discounts • Interact with our authors
in live broadcasts • Celebrate the cycle of the seasons with us
• Watch free videos from your favourite authors •
Connect with like-minded souls*

'*The gateways to wisdom and knowledge
are always open.*'

**Louise Hay**